Guides to Youth Ministry

EVANGELIZATION

Guides to Youth Ministry

EVANGELIZATION

Edited by
REYNOLDS R. EKSTROM

THE WORLD OF
DON BOSCO
MULTIMEDIA

New Rochelle, NY

Guide to Youth Ministry: Evangelization
is published as a service for adults who love the young
and want to share the Gospel with them.

It is a guide to understanding the young and a resource book for helping them.
As such, it is addressed to parish youth ministers, clergy who work with
the young, and teachers.

Other *Guides to Youth Ministry* available:

Retreats

Early Adolescent Ministry

Spirituality

Justice

Leadership

Liturgy and Worship

Media and Culture

Pastoral Care

Prepared in collaboration with The Center for Youth Ministry Development

Cover layout by J.P. Graphics

Composition by John Reinhardt Book Design

Guide to Youth Ministry: Leadership
© 1995 Don Bosco Multimedia
      130 Main Street, New Rochelle, NY 10801-5324
      All rights reserved

Library of Congress Cataloging-in-Publication Data
Evangelization/Reynolds R. Ekstrom
   p. cm.—(Guides to Youth Ministry)
   Includes biographical references
      1. Evangelization   2. Youth—Religious Life
   I. Ekstrom, Reynolds R.   II. Evangelization   III. Series

ISBN 0–89944–321–4

Printed in the United States of America

5/95   9 8 7 6 5 4 3 2 1

CONTENTS

ABOUT THE AUTHORS

REYNOLDS R. EKSTROM holds a master's degree in Pastoral Studies from Loyola of the South. He has been a staff member of the Center For Youth Ministry Development, and before that served as Associate Director of Religious Education for eight years in the Archdiocese of New Orleans. He is author of the *Concise Catholic Dictionary* (23rd Publications) and has edited *Guides to Youth Ministry: Evangelization, Access Guides to Youth Ministry: Retreats, Access Guides to Youth Ministry: Media and Culture,* and *TeenMedia.* He is a regular contributor to the journal *Top Music Countdown* and to the lectionary-based catechetical magazine called *SPIRIT.* He resides in New Orleans, Louisiana.

GILBERTO GAVAZOS, OFM is presently working on a doctorate in Spirituality at the Pontifical Institute of St. Anthony in Rome. Throughout his studies and ministry he has specialized in youth evangelization. He was parochial vicar and then pastor of Nuestra Senora de los Angeles in San Antonio for eight years. During that time he founded La Tropa de Cristo, a Franciscan Youth Evangelization Team.

ROBERT HATER, a priest of the Archdiocese of Cincinnati, is a professor of religious studies at the University of Dayton. He specializes in evangelization, catechesis, and ministry; and is an internationally known lecturer and author. Among his books are *News That is Good: Evangelization for Catholics* (Ave Maria Press).

ELIZABETH JOHNSON is associate professor of theology at Fordham University. She is the author of *Consider Jesus* (Crossroads) and several highly acclaimed articles. She is a frequent speaker at gatherings of religious educators, preachers, and pastoral and campus ministers.

JEFF JOHNSON was Director of Youth Ministry for the Archdiocese of St. Paul/Minneapolis. Jeff was a leader in youth evangelization, writing and giving workshops across the country, before his untimely death. His article appeared in the first edition of the *Guide* and is reprinted with slight modifications by the editor.

JOHN ROBERTO is Director and co-founder of the Center for Youth Ministry Development (USA). He teaches youth ministry and family faith development courses and institutes at universities and dioceses across the country. John has authored *The Leadership Development Program, Planning a Youth Ministry Resource Manual* and *Volunteer Leadership Resource Manual*, and co-authored with Tom East *Guides to Youth Ministry: Leadership* (DBM publications). He has served as editor for several Don Bosco Multimedia youth ministry publications, and has served as author and editor for the Catholic Families Series (DBM).

DONALD SENIOR is president of Catholic Theological Union, Chicago. He is the author of numerous books and articles and serves as associate editor of *The Bible Today* and *New Theology Review*, general editor of The Catholic Study Bible (Oxford University Press), and co-editor of the international commentary series, *New Testament Messages*. He has lectured and conducted retreats and workshops throughout the United States and abroad.

ACKNOWLEDGMENTS

"Jesus: The Center of Catholic Evangelization" originally appeared as Chapter 4 in *Consider Jesus* by Elizabeth A. Johnson (1990). Used by permission of Crossroads Publishing Company.

"Distinctive Qualities of Catholic Evangelization" by Robert Hater is reprinted from *The New Catholic Evangelization* edited by Kenneth Boyack, CSP (1992). Used by permission of Paulist Press.

INTRODUCTION

THE CHALLENGE OF EVANGELIZING YOUTH TODAY

EVANGELIZATION. The word alone brings fear and confusion to many. We often carry images of television evangelists, fundamentalist preachers, revival meetings, and church membership campaigns about "evangelization." Such images can cloud our appreciation for the place of Christian evangelization in our ministries with adolescents. Evangelization, after all, is the very heart of an effective, comprehensive ministry with youth. In this volume of the *Guides to Youth Ministry*, we have developed solid foundations and creative, practical approaches for Catholic evangelization which can provide direction to Catholics and others who wish to engage in faith-sharing among adolescents.

This *Guide* embraces the dual understandings of evangelization which come to us from contemporary church teachings and practice. Evangelization can be viewed as the *energizing core* of everything we do in youth ministry. In such light, each relationship formed and each ministry activity undertaken seeks to draw young people more deeply into a lifestyle characterized by Christian discipleship—following Jesus Christ and living the Good News of Christ in a conscious, active way. Viewing evangelization in a broad sense makes our whole ministry evangelizing and makes each one of us evangelizers.

However, in addition to being the energizing core of all of youth ministry, evangelization is also one *essential component* of any comprehensive approach to ministry with youth today. In this view, evangelization is a dynamic process involving outreach, invitation, gospel proclamation, and a call to Christian conversion. Whether you find yourself ministering in a parish, a school, or another setting, in our day, there are many young people who need yet to experience the healing and redemptive presence of Jesus, who need to learn better how to follow him, and who need to learn how the gospel of Jesus speaks to the various questions, pains, struggles, and joys in their lives. It is imperative that our efforts to do this kind of evangelization be strengthened today!

As you use this *Guide*, you will also notice that it addresses a number of difficult questions about the content of Catholic evangelization. Two important questions need to be surfaced and resolved regarding current youth evangelization efforts. Which images, or portraits, of Jesus of Nazareth are we going to use in order to invite adolescents into a meaningful relationship with him? And which elements of the gospel are we going to actively proclaim to young people? In our efforts to do effective outreach and proclamation of the Good News, the church's ministers sometimes edit gospel portraits in order to make Jesus and his timeless challenge safe and acceptable to all. We often, for instance, invite young people into relationship with a Jesus who is a friend and companion—emphasizing all those gifts Jesus gives humanity, like love, comfort, peace—but neglect to mention that Jesus requires his disciples (yes, disciples today) to lose their lives in order to find Life, to love enemies, to work for justice, and to embrace the Christian values of personal sacrifice and service. This book should challenge those who use it to ask if we fear, today, to really tell young people and others the whole gospel story and to proclaim all that Jesus demands of us because we fear that if we really lay it all out many with whom we work will turn and go the other way. The task of evaluating the content of our gospel proclamations with the full and authentic gospel message poses a great but daunting challenge for the contemporary evangelizer of adolescents, a challenge nevertheless which will keep us growing in Christian faith.

Together with the *Youth Evangelization Resource Manual*, which contains practical strategies and activities, this *Guide* provides an excellent introduction to the theory and practical of Catholic youth evangelization.

This *Guide* can also serve as a commentary on **The Challenge of Catholic Youth Evangelization** developed by the National Federation for Catholic Youth Ministry (published by DBM). Each essay in this volume provides further depth to a section of **The Challenge of Catholic Youth Evangelization.**

The Challenge of Catholic Youth Evangelization	*Guides to Youth Ministry: Evangelization*
Section 1: The Challenge	Chapter 1: Distinctive Qualities of Catholic Evangelization
Section 2: Foundations	Chapter 2: Jesus: The Center of Catholic Evangelization
	Chapter 3: Following Jesus: Discipleship Today
	Chapter 4: The Spiritual Hungers of America's Youth
Section 3: Principles	
Section 4: Dynamics	Chapter 3: Following Jesus: Discipleship Today
	Chapter 5: Proclaiming the Good News Today
	Chapter 6: Dynamics of Catholic Youth Evangelization
Section 5: Integration	Chapter 7: Integrating Evangelization Strategies into the Components of Comprehensive Youth Ministry
Section 6: Community	Chapter 8: The Evangelizing Community: Partnership in Evangelization of Adolescents
	Chapter 9: Empowering Adult Leaders for Evangelization
	Chapter 10: Empowering Adolecents for Evangelization

This *Guide*, like its companion Resource Manual, is meant to challenge those who use it to wonder if we fear, today, to tell young people and others the whole Gospel story and to share with them all that the Gospel demands of us because we fear if we really lay it all out many with whom we work will not be converted toward Christianity but will turn and go the other way. The task of examining and evaluating our own Gospel witness, outreach, and Christian (verbal) proclamations in light of the full and authentic Gospel message poses a great but exciting challenge for the contemporary evangelizer of adolescents. We hope, though, this is a challenge that will be aided by this resource manual and a challenge that will keep both you and its creators growing in faith.

INTRODUCTION TO
PART ONE

THE FOUNDATIONS OF CATHOLIC EVANGELIZATION

PART ONE OF THIS *GUIDE* begins with an essay by **Rev. Bob Hater** on the distinctive qualities and characteristics of Catholic evangelization. Using a number of personal stories and other vignettes, Fr. Hater explores the history of Christian evangelization, the meaning of the term "evnagelization," and the relationship between evangelization and our ultimate Christian mission, known as the kingdom or reign of God. To bring his essay to a close, he elaborates on ten particular qualities of Catholic evangelization and notes how these contribute to our work to share the Christian gospel with those persons and institutions we find in contemporary U.S. culture—a culture both blessed and materialistic—in our day.

Elizabeth Johnson reflects on the center of all genuine evangelization efforts, Jesus Christ. In a stirring meditation on the story of Jesus of Nazareth, she examines his "inspiring preaching" and various characteristics of his outreach to others. She goes on to investigate his mysterious death and resurrection and what these say about Jesus' "intimate, close, and tremendously compassionate" experience of the Creator, whom he called *Abba* ("papa"). This chapter concludes with implications that should be drawn, by those who would evangelize others as Christ's followers today, from the dynamic message and ministry of Jesus.

The theme of following Jesus—in other words, Christian discipleship—is taken up, again, in the next chapter of Part One, a chapter authored by **Rev. Donald Senior**. Fr. Senior invites us to look at the fundamentals of Christian discipleship, indicating that it is a personal call to follow Jesus, an experience of *metanoia*, an experience of community, and, at its root, a mission to go "fishing for people" who also will follow the Risen One. He conlcudes his piece with a reflection on the distinctive characteristics of Christian discipleship. Fr. Senior, in particular, notes that Christian life is both a grace, a spirited response to the message (story) of Jesus, and, most remarkably, at its best, an empowerment to walk the same journey as Jesus of Nazareth and all who have followed him over the ages.

The next chapter is written by **Reynolds R. Ekstrom**, and he looks at the spiritual hungers of the adolescents in the U.S. today. Indicating that the present time is ripe for an all-encompassing effort, by the adult community in general, and by Christian churches in specific, to respond to the spiritual and moral needs of young people, he names the spiritual hungers of youth in our day and offers suggestions on how to allay them-through the implementation of a "preferential option for youth" in our local communities. This chapter explains that the spiritual needs of adolescents, in the 1990s, which will only continue to grow—unless dealt with effectively in the near futuere—are a hunger for meaningful relationships and structures, a hunger for good listeners, a hunger for justice and a chance to serve others.

Part One is brought to a conclusion by an essay by **John Roberto** on proclaiming the Good News to youth today in response to the hungers outlined in the *Challenge* document and the essay by Reynolds Ekstrom.

CHAPTER 1

DISTINCTIVE QUALITIES OF CATHOLIC EVANGELIZATION

ROBERT J. HATER

*Evangelization has two fundamental meanings: First of all, evangelization is the **initial effort** by the faith community as a whole to proclaim through word and witness the Good News of the Gospel to those who have not yet heard or seen it, and then to invite those persons into a relationship with Jesus Christ and the community of believers.*

*Second, evangelization is the **ongoing** witness of the faith community as it attempts to live out the Gospel with such authenticity that the faith of all the members is sustained and nourished. As such, evangelization is recognized as the energizing core of the life of the church, and all its ministries: word, sacrament, all forms of pastoral ministry, and justice and service.*

—The Challenge of Catholic Youth Evangelization

A PARISHIONER RECENTLY COMMENTED, "Why are Catholics now discussing evangelization? That's for Protestants, not us." Actually, the contrary is true. Evangelization forms the heart of Catholic life and mission.

Catholic evangelization begins before people come to church. A childhood story illustrates this point:

> Our family eagerly awaited Thanksgiving dinner on a warm November day. My sister, Mary Ann (age 5) and I (age 6) heard the doorbell ring and ran to answer it. A boy (about 10) and a girl (about 11) asked for money. The girl held a baby covered with a light blanket. We called Mom. The girl said, "We are poor and have not money for food. Please give us some money."
>
> Mom told them that we did not have much money, but we had plenty of food. We offered to share Thanksgiving dinner with them. The children hesitated. Then Mom said she would make three meals for them to take along. The children said, "Okay."
>
> Dad, Mary Ann and I helped Mom prepare the containers of food. We gladly shared our food with these less fortunate children. They accepted the food and left. Mary Ann and I watched them walk up the street.
>
> When the children got to the corner, the girl threw the baby to the boy. He tossed it up and down. We called Mom. She came quickly to see what was happening. Then the children tossed the food down the sewer, laughed and disappeared around the corner.
>
> Mary Ann and I cried, thinking they hurt the baby. We cried harder when they threw the food down the sewer.
>
> Mom called us to her and said, "I have something important to tell you. That wasn't a baby; it was a doll. The children tricked us. They only wanted money. But we will have a fine Thanksgiving, for we gave with a good heart. That's the most important thing. The value of a gift doesn't depend on whether someone appreciates it. It's value comes because we gave out of love. God will bless us because of our gift. God gave his Son, Jesus, and people rejected him. Our gift of food is like God's gift of Jesus."
>
> We had a great Thanksgiving, one I will never forget.[1]

Was my mother an evangelizer? The answer to this question depends on one's view of evangelization, for Catholic evangelization differs from Protestant, fundamentalist evangelism. This essay explores these differences.

MEANING OF CATHOLIC EVANGELIZATION

Catholic Church documents describe holistic and restricted views of evangelization. The *wide* or *holistic* view is reflected in "On Evangelization in the Modern World" (*Evangelii Nuntiandi*) and in "On Catechesis in Our Time" (*Catechesi Tradendae*). Seen in this way, *evangelization is an ongoing conversion process within the Christian community, a process that seeks to initiate people ever more deeply into the mystery of God's love (i.e., the kingdom), as it is manifested most fully in the dying and rising of Jesus.*

This evangelization process, inspired by the Spirit, is a response to God's call to proclaim the good news of the kingdom in word and deed. Mom proclaimed this message to Mary Ann and me on Thanksgiving by teaching about the real meaning of a gift. Business executives can evangelize in corporate board rooms. This is not a special vocation but one central to the Christian calling. Evangelization is part of a lifelong conversion process in which God's word is heard again and again. Seeing evangelization in this wide, holistic sense, my mother was an evangelizer on that Thanksgiving Day.

Evangelization is the lifeblood of Christian life and ministry. As an ongoing activity of the community, it includes the initial proclamation of the word, as well as various pastoral ministries which nourish this initial proclamation. Hence, various ministries (catechesis, liturgy, service activities) contribute to the church's evangelizing activity. The chief ministries of word, worship and service are key aspects of evangelization (Figure 1).

Family, Church and world have vital roles to play in evangelization. The Church must relate to family and world as subjects, not objects, of evangelization. The latter are not objects "out there" to be evangelized, with little to contribute to the dialogue. Evangelization means communicating among subjects, each manifesting a different face of God (Figure 2).

The *General Catechetical Directory*, the *National Catechetical Directory* and the Rite of Christian Initiation of Adults (RCIA) propose a *more restricted* view of evangelization. These documents describe evangelization (and sometimes pre-evangelization) as operative before a person makes

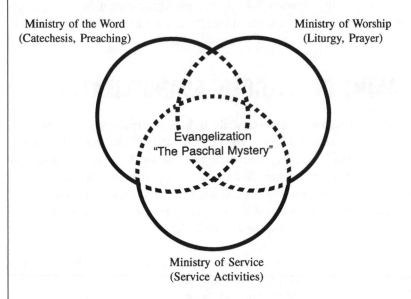

Figure 1
Distinctive Qualities of Catholic Evangelization

Ministry of the Word
(Catechesis, Preaching)

Ministry of Worship
(Liturgy, Prayer)

Evangelization
"The Paschal Mystery"

Ministry of Service
(Service Activities)

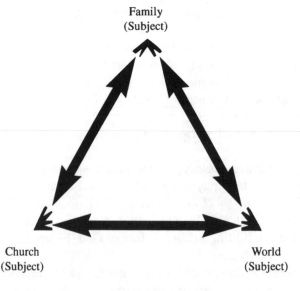

Figure 2
The New Catholic Evangelization

Family
(Subject)

Church
(Subject)

World
(Subject)

a faith commitment. Evangelization is seen in terms of the initial proclamation of the gospel, which is directed toward conversion and is followed
by catechesis. In this sense, people are evangelized before and catechized
after their faith commitment.

Catholics today are opting for the holistic view of evangelization, also
called the "convergence" model of evangelization. Both Catholic views
differ from a more fundamentalist approach which emphasizes hearing the
word of God and accepting Jesus Christ once and for all, in a definite
moment of being converted or saved.

In proclaiming the lived reality of Jesus' dying, rising and sending of
the Spirit, evangelization energizes Christian endeavors, reminding Christians of their mission to live out God's kingdom message. Christian life is
rooted in the life-blood and marrow of evangelization. Without it, individual or institutional efforts to proclaim God's word, celebrate it, or serve
others lack the dynamism promised by the good news.

EVANGELIZATION AND THE KINGDOM OF GOD

What is the good news that Jesus proclaimed? Answering this question
involves the heart of the Christian message, namely, the kingdom of God.
All evangelization centers around this message.

Jesus' kingdom message is reflected clearly in his words in the Nazareth
synagogue, "He has sent me to bring good news to the poor, to proclaim
liberty to captives and to the blind new sight, to set the down-trodden free,
to proclaim the Lord's year of favor" (Lk 4:18–19).

Jesus proclaimed the good news of the kingdom and promised peace in
this life and blessedness in the next for those who follow him. In so doing,
Jesus is the model for all evangelization.

The Christian scriptures reveal the components of Jesus' evangelizing activities. In his apostolic exhortation "On Evangelization in the Modern World,"
Pope Paul VI describes them as Jesus' incarnation, his miracles, his teaching,
the gathering of the disciples, the sending out of the twelve, the crucifixion and
resurrection, and the permanence of his presence in the Christian community
(nn. 6–13). These seven components remind Christians that evangelization is
much more than "words." It presupposes the witness of faith, hope and charity.

Pope Paul VI describes two distinctive yet related aspects of Jesus' evangelizing activity: the kingdom of God and liberating salvation (nn. 8-9). Mark links these activities by quoting Jesus, "The time has come . . . and the kingdom of God is close at hand. Repent and believe the good news" (Mk 1:15). To embrace the kingdom, repentance is necessary, for a person's relationship to the kingdom is linked with liberation from sin. The church's Ash Wednesday liturgy implies this connection in the words used while ashes are administered, "Turn away from sin and be faithful to the gospel."

The Christian community continues Jesus' mission and ministry which focuses on the kingdom. Christian efforts make little sense if their dynamism does not reflect the kingdom. To ensure fidelity to Jesus' command the church receives the Spirit, whose actions are discerned in light of scripture, tradition and magisterial interpretations.

An event at Eastertime challenged me to look more deeply into the meaning of evangelization. It happened during the Good Friday liturgy.

> St. Clare parishioners narrated the passion account in words and actions. I sat on the side of the church, reflecting on the gospel story, when suddenly Jesus' words to Pilate, "Mine is not a kingdom of this world" (Jn 18:36), pierced my soul. This expression struck me as it never did before.
>
> In a few moments, I stood beside the life-size cross that I had just carried up the aisle to the altar. I began my homily, "Mine is not a kingdom of this world."
>
> These words remained with me, as later I reflected on the biblical understanding of the kingdom of God.

No description adequately expresses Jesus' teaching on the kingdom of God. Some people translate it as the reign, rule or sovereignty of God. Others prefer the presence of God. The latter is appealing because God's kingdom is wherever God is present. It is an action, not an abstract concept.

Although the kingdom of God is elusive and paradoxical, it has several levels of meaning, rooted in Jesus' words, "Mine is not a kingdom of this world."

Jesus believed in the imminent coming of God's kingdom, seen as a radical, even cataclysmic event. He taught the disciples to get ready for its arrival. When he called Peter, Andrew, James and John, he said, "The time has come and the kingdom of God is close at hand" (Mk 1:15). His death must come first, and his resurrection would testify to the immediate coming of the kingdom. After Jesus' ascension the disciples waited anxiously for his return in glory to initiate this kingdom.

Jesus also announced the kingdom's presence on earth in his role as a servant. He taught that God is present now, working to heal the broken and forgive the sinners. Paul reflects this by saying, " . . . because the kingdom does not mean eating or drinking this or that, it means righteousness and peace and joy brought by the Holy Spirit" (Rom 14:20).

Jesus predicted his resurrection; it happened. He also spoke of the imminent coming of the kingdom; it did not happen. In this mystery rests the great unfinished symphony of Christianity and its greatest paradox. If belief in Jesus' resurrection requires faith, belief in his second coming requires absolute faith.

Consequently, to appreciate the kingdom of God means to live the kingdom "now" through ministry to economically, psychologically, spiritually and physically poor people. This focuses on healing, forgiveness and reconciliation of weak, sinful people, while anticipating the future kingdom of God.

This future kingdom, which Jesus predicted, has a universal, communitarian scope. It is not limited to the union of a person with God in the afterlife. It is for all good people. When it comes, heaven and earth will be transformed. Then all members of God's kingdom will rise from the dead, as Jesus did, and a new era will begin.

The kingdom of God means God's radical presence here on earth, yet always beyond this world. It is mysterious, transcendent, and can best be described in stories and parables. When Christians lose sight of the apocalyptic aspect of the kingdom and regard it as some king of "heaven on earth," or stress "what is to come" and neglect the "now," they miss the full dynamism of Jesus' message.

A balanced stance for Christians in God's unfinished symphony involves living with faith in a paradoxical world of sin and tension.

The Catholic view of the kingdom shows how the evangelist John, near the end of his life, after waiting for Jesus' second coming, gave his disciples a symbolic blueprint for faith in the book of Revelation. This book is the final piece of the kingdom's paradox, which always reminds Christians of the need for faith in a mysterious, yet loving God.

Catholic evangelization must always maintain belief in God's radical presence and the consequent process of the overcoming of sin. Any other posture means living on the surface of Christianity, never probing its depth.

EVANGELIZATION AND CONTEMPORARY CULTURE

Jesus proclaimed the good news of God's kingdom within a Jewish culture. Early Christians reinterpreted his message within a broader culture (Greek, Roman, African and more). Today, United States Catholics struggle to refocus Jesus' teaching in a materialistic, technological world.

"Culture" is viewed here from a double vantage point, namely United States culture and world culture. Both perspectives offer significant challenges for Catholic evangelization.

United States Culture

The mix of wealth and poverty in United States culture bears many resemblances to the culture of Jesus' time. Gradually the middle class is thinning out, as the gulf widens between rich and poor. At the same time, technological advances offer many promises for the future. The current situation brings blessings and challenges to the Catholic evangelist.

On the *positive* side, contemporary culture presents wonderful blessings, such as television, radio, rapid transportation, computers and suchlike. These make possible advances in medicine, health care, food production and worldwide distribution of goods. The Catholic evangelist recognizes God's presence in these scientific developments.

The *negative* side of modern culture includes greed, materialism, immorality, secularization of values, and the abuse of technology. Today's evangelist must face the great challenge of a sinful, hedonistic world and challenge it with gospel values. The kingdom message can never be accommodated to materialistic culture without destroying the spirit of Jesus' teachings.

World Culture²

Jesus' kingdom is broader than the church; it exists wherever God's presence is manifested. Consequently, wherever people strive to live good, upright lives, regardless of their religion or culture, God's kingdom exists.

Jesus' first disciples were Jewish, but soon his message spread to the Gentile world. At the Council of Jerusalem (50 A.D.) Christianity was liberated from the Jewish culture, and no longer were Christians obliged to observe Hebrew rituals, like circumcision or dietary laws, to be faithful disciples of Jesus. Gradually, his message was reinterpreted within various cultures (African, Asian, Roman). In time the western cultural model took over, as terms like substance, nature and person replaced Hebrew expressions. For nineteen hundred years westernized Christianity predominated. Christian missionaries brought it to other cultures and changed them in light of western ways.

Vatican II effected a major shift in acknowledging God's presence among all great world religions and cultures (e.g., Buddhism, Islam, Judaism). No longer can a westernized form of Christianity be imposed upon other cultures. Future Christianity will be changed in light of non-western cultures as Buddhism, Islam and native religions bring fresh insights to Christianity. Just as westernization changed Jewish Christianity, so will world cultures bring new insights, vocabulary and spirit to contemporary Christian understandings of Jesus and the kingdom.

Catholic evangelization must acknowledge the rich soil of dialogue inherent in world cultures, as they begin to interact more dialogically within western Christianity.

DISTINCTIVE QUALITIES OF CATHOLIC EVANGELIZATION

The meaning and history of evangelization and its relationship to kingdom and culture imply ten distinctive qualities of Catholic evangelization.

1. Catholic evangelization is rooted in life itself.

Evangelization begins in the *family* (integral, divorced, single parent). Witnessing my family's live through a lifetime taught me how birth, growth, joy, sorrow, success, failure, life and death root human relationships with God. Families are challenged to see their critical role in God's plan of evangelizing all people.

The *world* (friends, workplace, technology, culture, neighbors, business offices, civic associations) can also reflect God's presence. At the same time it can lead people away from God, for today's amoral, materialistic culture is the greatest challenge to Christian faith.

Catholic evangelization invites all Christians to see their work as a vital aspect of their calling by God and to respond to this calling by evangelizing their workplace through good example, just business practices and wholesome, moral conduct.

The *Church* plays a special role in evangelization. Parishioners gather to hear God's word, celebrate liturgy, pray, learn, support one another, and serve needy people. When family evangelization is absent, other Christians can significantly influence children, youth and adults. Many people are Christians today because a friend, teacher or church minister encouraged them. Breakdowns in many families today—drugs, divorce, latchkey children—indicate that Catholic evangelization within the Church must focus strong efforts on the family.

2. Catholic evangelization is directed toward the kingdom of God.

The goal of evangelization is to share faith, and, in so doing, to further God's kingdom of charity, justice and mercy. The Church helps bring God's kingdom to completion. Whenever Christians support, love and forgive hurting people, God's kingdom is present.

Catholic evangelization acknowledges Jesus' unfinished symphony, knowing that someday he will come again, and that believers will rise from the dead as he did. This radical awareness calls Christians to live their everyday lives in God's mystery as their absolute future. At the same time, Catholic evangelization acknowledges God's presence in other Christian denominations, world religions and culture. It sees the need to reinterpret the Christian message within these cultures, as the planet moves closer to becoming a world culture.

3. Catholic evangelization is always related in some way to the Christian community.

Catholic evangelization presupposes a communal aspect and never reflects the "me and Jesus" focus of many TV evangelists. Catholics believe that God calls them as a people to follow Jesus. Usually this begins in the family and last a lifetime.

Evangelization that does not include a communal aspect is one-sided and incomplete. Community creates a climate where people feel at home, supported and able to appreciate the presence of God's spirit in their everyday lives.

Evangelization, however, includes more than participating in church-related ministries, inviting lapsed Catholics back to church, and welcoming new church members. It includes all activities directed to the kingdom of God.

4. Catholic evangelization recognizes all church members as partners in furthering God's kingdom.

God's spirit is manifested most fully in a healthy relationship between laity, sisters, brothers, priests, pastoral ministers, deacons, theologians, bishops and the pope. The Catholic approach to evangelization acknowledges different yet complementary gifts existing in the church.

Jesus' work on earth continues through all Church members under the guidance of the magisterium. A healthy give-and-take within the entire Church community guarantees fidelity to God's revelation and avoids one-sided interpretations, sometimes characteristic of individual-centered evangelists.

5. Catholic evangelization energizes Christian activities and church ministries.

Rooted in God's kingdom, Catholic evangelization provides dynamism for the ministries of word, worship and service. These ministries are aspects or moments in the evangelization process; each presupposes initial acts of evangelization occurring in the family, workplace or Church.

These ministries merge at many points and cannot function effectively apart from one another. Catechesis, liturgy and social activities, for example, interpenetrate one another, although they focus respectively within the context of the ministries of word, worship and service.

Catholic evangelization is one process with many aspects which become one dynamic whole. To evangelize as through proclaiming God's word has little or no relationship to prayer, eucharist, community worship or social concern is not the "Catholic" way. Evangelization efforts flow from the paschal mystery and are unified in a holistic vision of God's word experienced and celebrated in a vibrant faith life.

Every church organization, structure and activity must help teach people God's word and celebrate life. Religious education/catechesis, liturgy, sacramental preparation programs and St. Vincent de Paul societies are good ways to evangelize. Concern for the poor and financial priorities speak volumes about a parish's commitment to evangelization.

"Welcome" is the first requirement for successful evangelization. Baptisms, funerals and weddings provide wonderful occasion to evangelize. Impersonal answering machines never enhance a parish's reputation as a welcome place.

Effective evangelization means all church ministers accept their call to further God's kingdom.

6. Catholic evangelization interprets scripture in a rich way and does not limit the Bible to its literal meaning.

Catholics accept the Bible as God's word, written in human language. The Bible includes literal accounts, poetry, parables, hymns, and such like. Catholic evangelization interprets biblical passages (e.g., Adam and Eve or magi stories) in light of why they were written, their literary forms (poetry, historical) and church tradition. Since a passage's meaning is not always clear, Catholics get help from Church tradition, magisterial teachings, and scholarly research.

Some biblical evangelists insist on the literal interpretation of all scripture passages. This approach is inadequate. It makes no more sense to interpret every scripture passage literally than to demand literal interpretation for every newspaper account (news, editorials, comics).

Catholic evangelization encourages people to study scripture, pray with it, and allow God's word to touch our lives.

7. Catholic evangelization is optimistic, but realistic.

Catholic evangelization believes that the world is basically good, but admits the presence of sin and evil. God created a good world. After sin entered the world (depicted in the Adam and Eve story), the world remained good but wounded.

Catholics reject evangelical efforts that say creation-after-the-fall is evil. This approach concentrates on sin and corruption and minimizes basic human goodness. While admitting sin's allurement, Catholic evangelization focuses on God's promise of hope and freedom.

8. Catholic evangelization is a lifelong journey to God.

Catholic evangelization is a continuous process, not a once-and-for-all event, as many TV evangelists claim.

Biblical evangelists say that conversion, a once-and-for-all event, happens when a person is "saved." While Catholic evangelization admits that one event (sickness, death, a joyous occasion) may trigger conversion, it teaches that conversion is a lifelong journey to god, not a single isolated event. On this journey both faith and good works are necessary for salvation.

9. Catholic evangelization happens in the midst of everyday living.

Catholic evangelization stresses the need to discover God in ordinary life. This happened when Mom taught Mary Ann and me the value of a gift on Thanksgiving. It can happen many times each day if people are open to God's presence in everyday life. Prayers such as the Morning Offering are excellent ways to acknowledge daily opportunities to share Christian faith.

10. Catholic evangelization offers a firm anchor and clear direction in an uncertain world.

Catholic evangelization gives people a two thousand year faith tradition, definite beliefs, deep spirituality and vibrant liturgical life. It does not shift with the latest whim. At the same time, while rooted in basic beliefs and practices, Catholic evangelization is ever fresh, because the Spirit constantly invites Christians to apply God's word, especially scripture, to their every-changing world. This means maintaining the basics of scripture, Catholic beliefs and practices, while remaining open to personal and cultural changes.

"Evangelization" is a Catholic word, deeply rooted in the Christian heritage. Our family's early Thanksgiving experience, and many like it, symbolizes the deep significance of evangelization. Just as our family was drawn closer on that day, so will God's help strengthen all people on their common journey to the kingdom of God.

End Notes

[1] This story originally appeared in my book, *Holy Family: Christian Families in a Changing World.* Allen, TX: Tabor Publishing, 1988. p. 67-68, and was adapted for this essay.

[2] See address given by Karl Rahner, "Towards a Fundamental Theological Interpretation of Vatican II," trans. Leo J. O'Donovan, SJ, *Theological Studies*, vol. 40, December 1987, p. 716-27.

CHAPTER 2

JESUS: THE CENTER OF CATHOLIC EVANGELIZATION

ELIZABETH JOHNSON

An understanding of Jesus' ministry and its applicability to the situation of young people today provides the foundation for effective Catholic youth evangelization.

"The Word became flesh/and made his dwelling among us" (Jn 1:14). Jesus is God and the fullest revelation of God, and his ways are the embodiment of God's ways in this world. Therefore, Jesus' ministry, death and resurrection are normative for our faith and are the source of our ministry. We are challenged to place the story of Jesus into dialogue with our own ministry, and certainly with our own lives and the lives of our young people.

—The Challenge of Catholic Youth Evangelization

WITHIN A HIGHLY STRUCTURED DOGMATIC FRAMEWORK, the first wave of renewal in Catholic christology occurred in the 1950s and 1960s when theologians pondered the dogmatic confession of Jesus Christ's identity. The insights that emerged pointed to a deeper appreciation of the genuine humanity of the Word made flesh, and of the dignity and value of every human being. The Second Vatican Council incorporated the results of much of this work and built on it. The council also took a step that was to be highly significant for developments in christology, namely, it approved the study of the scriptures using modern historical and critical methods. As a result, Catholic biblical scholarship came into its own, and the gospels began to be studied as never before.

The second wave of renewal in Catholic christology formed and swelled as a direct result. Theologians now began christology by reflecting not on the Chalcedonian dogma but on the scriptural stories and testimony about Jesus Christ, leading to ideas which have a concrete and historical flavor to them. The questions which now arise concern not his human nature, divine nature, and one hypostasis, but his life's story: What was he like as a real person in history? What did he stand for? How did he make such an impact? Why did the authorities consider him dangerous? Why was he crucified?

Starting in the late 1960s and flowering in the 1970s this approach was followed by theologians such as Karl Rahner in his later years, Edward Schillebeeckx (still working on the third volume of his trilogy on Jesus Christ), Hans Kung, Walter Kasper, Gerald O'Collins, James Mackey, Monika Hellwig, William Thompson, and many others. The guiding motivation of their work springs from Christian faith with a turn to the practical. If God became a human being, and this is what the first wave of renewal emphasized, then it is very important to see what kind of human being God became. If Jesus is God with us, then his story is an answer to the question, "Who is God?" If Jesus is the revelation of God and stood for definite purposes and upheld certain values, then the significance of that for believers is inestimable. What he does, in the concrete, matters; it embodies the way of God in this world which patterns our way as disciples today. In other words, Jesus does not just have a human nature in the abstract, but a very concrete human history. We need to put *that* story into dialogue with our own lives today.

What results is a narrative christology. Its method is to uncover the story of Jesus in history and then to correlate this story with the situation of the community of disciples today. When contemporary biblical scholarship studies the gospels, what emerges as of first-rate importance is the ministry of Jesus. It is interesting that for centuries Catholic christology did not deal with Jesus' adult activities very extensively, but focused its attention on his birth and death. If you doubt this, just think of the traditional mysteries of the Rosary, where meditation skips from the joyful to the sorrowful mysteries without lingering over what happened in between. The second wave of renewal has recovered the historical ministry as intrinsically important to christology.

There is a shift taking place here, from a christology "from above" to a christology "from below." In John's gospel, in patristic and medieval christology, as well as in the first wave of renewal which grappled with the dogma about Jesus Christ, thought begins in heaven, "above." Starting with the belief that this is the Word of God, we trace his descent into our world, marveling at the love of God which impels such identification with us and our troubles. In the christology of the synoptic gospels (Matthew, Mark, and Luke), as well as in this second wave of renewal which seeks to tell the story of Jesus, though begins on earth, "below." Starting with the concrete memories of Jesus of Nazareth and his impact, we trace his ascent through death and resurrection to the glory of God, challenged to follow his way in our own lives as a believing community. In this approach, Jesus is named first of all a prophet and messenger from God — and more than a prophet; the greatest of the prophets; the eschatological prophet who brings the final word from God into the world, a word of compassionate and liberating love.

Thinking about Jesus Christ first of all from the scriptures has led to a practical, narrative christology which places the story of Jesus in critical correlation with the lives of believers today. The story involves three moments: ministry, death, resurrection. The ministry in turn is comprised of three elements: his preaching, characteristic way of behaving, and manner of relating to God. Finally, the correlation takes place in three ways, as the church believes, acts, and theorizes upon the story of Jesus.

MINISTRY: PREACHING

Jesus was an inspired preacher, filled with the Holy Spirit. The word of God burned in him and attracted others as he proclaimed it. What did he preach? His focus was not on extended doctrines, or on himself, his significance and identity. Rather, at the heart of his preaching was the symbol of the reign of God. Taken from the Hebrew tradition this symbol signifies what the state of affairs will be when God is recognized as the One on whom everyone sets their hearts, when God finally reigns. The kingdom of God is *God* getting the divine way unopposed by human sinfulness and the powers of darkness. On that day everyone will do what God wants, the will of God will be done on earth. In the Lord's Prayer we say, "Thy kingdom come, They will be done on earth as it is in heaven," and we are asking for the same thing in two different ways. The reign of God is the situation that results when God's will is really done. What is God's will? As revealed in Jesus, God's will is our well-being. God wants the wholeness, the healing, and the salvation of every creature and of all of us taken together. The reign of God, then, involves justice and peace among everyone, healing and wholeness everywhere, fullness of life enjoyed by all. It is what the scriptures call the situation of *shalom*, peace experienced not only as the absence of war but peace as the fullness of life. God wills this to come, God wants the world to be this way. In the prophets there are many beautiful images which evoke this reign of God: the lion lying down with the lamb (the strong not eating up the weak); soldiers beating war instruments into farming instruments; a marvelous harvest; a wedding feast with food enough for everyone and joy all around. All of these images could be supplemented by pictures of life today. What would the reign of God be like in urban images, in images taken from life in the United States, in Central American images, in Palestinian images, in South African images? What values would prevail? It is a reign of justice and peace, the fullness of life for every single person.

Jesus' preaching was shaped by the tradition of Judaism which was hoping for the reign of God, expecting that the reign of God would come at the last day when God came to judge the living and the dead and set up the kingdom of justice and peace. A new and burning sense that this reign is *near* pervades his preaching. The first words out of his mouth in Mark's gospel proclaim, "The time has come; the kingdom is near. Repent and believe in the good news." (Mk 1:15). What Jesus is announcing is that we do not have to wait until the last day for *shalom* to arrive, but God is already drawing near with salvation for all. It is dawning, it is breaking in, it is already starting to happen. The reign of God is at hand; salvation is on its way from God. This message is very urgent. There is an excitement about Jesus' preaching, a sense of anticipation as God approaches to heal and to save. And what must we do? Repent and believe in the good news. Turn our heart around, open up, be converted, and believe the good news. This *is* good news if it is true. It is great news that the reign of God is near instead of far away on the last day. I have sometimes asked my students, "What is good about the good news?" And I have not often received much of an answer, because religion seems kind of grim and dutiful and serious. It is anything but that in the preaching of Jesus. The symbol of the reign of God flowers in his imagination as the good news that God, powerful and compassionate, is coming close and wills to save, to establish justice and peace for all. This is what Jesus preaches in hundreds of different ways. Many of his parables begin, "the reign of God is like"; as the stories unfold, there is always a twist somewhere that leaves us wondering. The parables show that the reign of God is going to be surprising; it is not going to involve business as usual. Values are going to be turned upside down, and people whom the world considered nonpersons will be first, brought especially into the center of the kingdom. This is indeed good news if you are one of the last, least, or lowest! The beatitudes of Jesus also reflect this: Blessed are the poor, those who mourn, those who hunger and thirst for justice, those who make peace, because theirs is the kingdom of heaven (Mt 5:3-12).

This message of the reign of God comes with a great challenge for those who will not repent and believe the good news. Woe to the rich, the overstuffed, the esteemed, to those who think they deserve the front seats, to those who oppress and bind heavy burdens on the back of the poor. When the reign of God comes, they are going to be cast out — unless they repent. This message has teeth in it; it is not all sweetness and light. There is always the option to repent, but it is a challenge to those who think they have got it made to open their minds and hearts and enter into the perspective of God toward the oppressed. The reign of justice and peace, the reign of *shalom*, the reign of God—this marvelous hope is at the heart of all of Jesus' preaching. He is possessed with it and its nearness.

MINISTRY: CHARACTERISTIC BEHAVIOR

Jesus did not just speak about the coming reign of God. In his own practical ways he enacted it. In the things he did it began to arrive, began to come about in people's lives. What kind of behavior was characteristic of him?

1. Jesus called disciples to follow him.

Women as well as men responded, leaving their families, their homes, their jobs, and their villages. They formed a community of brothers and sisters around him, traveling with him, listening to him and being taught by him, learning his ways and even being sent on mission by him, little trial runs into ministry while he was still with them. After Jesus' death and resurrection, this band of followers formed the nucleus of the church.

2. He showed partisanship for the marginal people of his society and did so in many, many ways.

He associated with sinners, offering them forgiveness. He frequently healed the sick, reaching out to touch them, and disputing the believe that sickness was a punishment for sin. By the power of God working through him Jesus restored *shalom* to their bodies and to their spirits. In the case of lepers and others whose sickness had ostracized them from the community, his cures brought them back into life-giving relationships with other human beings. Jesus also exorcised demons, struggling with the power of evil; again, through him the power of God overcame evil and brought the afflicted back into harmony with God, with their own spirits, and so with others. Over and over again, Jesus typically searched for and reached out to the marginal lives of his society, to people suffering physically, spiritually, and socially, giving them a taste of the joy of the kingdom's arrival. In a particular way, his ministry shows the triumph of God's will over the forces that bind people who are considered of no account.

3. Jesus shared companionship both with his disciples and with the wider circle of those interested in him.

Religious art has focused on the Last Supper, but indeed it was only the last of a whole history of suppers that Jesus had with "his own" and with others. In the culture of the Middle East, sitting down at table with someone and breaking bread sets up a real bond of kinship. Not done lightly, this action makes people into friends, colleagues, "family." What Jesus did was to sit down at table with all manner of folks, including sinners, tax collectors, prostitutes, people considered nonentities and outside the reign of God in every way. They would break bread together after his preaching, after many people had been healed and forgiven, celebrating their return to one another. People found themselves at the table with Jesus in a new kind of community, sharing with people they never thought they would sit down with. A foretaste of the kingdom of God is savored at these joyful meals, where Jesus is guest of honor or host. No doubt the wine flowed freely at these suppers, for Jesus is accused by the Pharisees of being a drunk and a glutton. In addition his disciples are criticized for not fasting as did John the Baptist's. This was a genuine historical criticism that stung. Not that Jesus was guilty as charged. But he was perceived as someone who made merry, and his meals were considered a bit uproarious, very joyful, a foretaste of the joy of the kingdom in its fullness. Edward Schillebeeckx, who deals at length with these suppers, makes an interesting point: At these meals, being sad in Jesus' presence is an existential impossibility. You just could not keep your own sadness in that kind of company. The reign of God is near, Jesus is its mediator, and as you get into his circle, the joy breaks out. This is not a superficial joy. It springs from a deep sense that persons are restored to their own dignity and peace before God, and there find themselves in a new community with one another. It is a foretaste of the kingdom of God.

4. Jesus is both faithful and free regarding the great Jewish tradition of Torah.

Raised in a religious household and taught to observe the Jewish customs and to pray the Jewish prayers, Jesus was a Jew, an observant Jew. But there were occasions when he broke the Torah, and that gave scandal. In every single case when the law was set aside, it was because the well-being of someone was at stake. In face of the sick, the suffering, and the hunger, the Sabbath observances were given second priority. This is how he interprets the Torah. When challenged as to what was the greatest commandment among the many of the Torah, his fundamental answer was to lift up two of them and make them one: "You shall love the Lord your God with all your heart and soul and mind and strength; and you shall love your neighbour as yourself." (Mt 22:37-39). In other words love is at the heart of the reign of God; not an easy love but a self-giving love on the model of God. Such love grounds the law, puts it in correct perspective, and fulfills it. Loving this way, Jesus himself creates a liberating life-style and shows a wonderful freedom to do good.

5. It is very clear in the gospels that Jesus' whole ministry was rooted in prayer.

In addition to the prescribed daily and feast-day Jewish prayers, Jesus also prayed with personal initiative. He would go out at night by himself to pray. He would also find time for his disciples to come away from the crowds now and then to reflect. He even taught them how to pray for the coming of God's reign. Running throughout his ministry was a very deep spirituality as source of the preaching and effective action in which he was involved.

MINISTRY: RELATIONSHIP TO GOD

From the way Jesus talked about God and enacted the reign of God, it is obvious that he had a special and original experience of God as intimate, close, and tremendously compassionate over human suffering and sin. Out of that experience Jesus surfaced a name for God, namely *Abba*. In the Hebrew scriptures God is occasionally called "Father" in some of the psalms and prophets. But *Abba* does not exactly mean Father. It is the Aramaic word that a small child would use to address his or her father before being able to talk. As such a babble word, it really translates into English as "papa" or "dada" or some other equivalent. Every language has these little words that children use before they can really speak, but which they can use to call on their nearest and dearest. Jesus' own personal experience of God as close and compassionate led him to name God in this very intimate way, *Abba*. The name evokes the power of a very close relationship between Jesus and the One he names this way. Furthermore, Jesus teaches others to call God *Abba*, encouraging them to trust God the way little children trust a good parent to take care of them, be compassionate over their weakness, and stand guard against those who would harm them. Jesus' *Abba* experience is the heart of the matter, the dynamism behind his preaching the reign of God and of his typical way of acting. God *Abba* was the passion of his life.

Death

In his historical approach, it becomes crystal clear that Jesus' death was not an accident. Rather, it was the price he paid for his ministry. First of all, Jesus triggered a great deal of conflict with the religious authorities of his day. He did not necessarily want this, but it was almost inevitable, given the preaching and activity that he was engaged in. He was standing for one interpretation of God and Torah in the face of another more official interpretation that was held by the religious leaders. The Jewish tradition came into conflict with itself. There was also a sense among these leaders, especially evident in some of the trial scenes, that the enthusiasm generated by Jesus' ministry was dangerous in a political sense. Crowds of people were following him and there could easily be an uprising, which would cause the Romans, the occupying military power, to devastate the land. Recall that famous scene where the high priest says it is better that one man should die for the people than that the Romans should come and burn all the cities (Jn 11:48–50). Thus, the leaders rejected him for religious reasons, actually accusing him during his trial of blasphemy, of claiming the authority to understand God better than the governing religious leaders themselves did. But they also worried about the political implication of his ministry and where that would lead, and decided they could not afford to leave him at large. In the face of that opposition, Jesus went ahead with his ministry, continuing freely in love, commitment, and fidelity; if he had chosen to opt out of his ministry he would not necessarily have ended up crucified. Events them took their rapid course. He was arrested, interrogated, tortured, and put to death. Historically, he died a failure. His message was rejected by many people; among his disciples one betrayed him, one denied even knowing him, most of the males abandoned him, although the women kept vigil at the cross; his ministry came to a screeching halt. He was executed in the prime of his life.

Worst of all, it seemed that even God, whom he had preached as compassionate and loving *Abba*, had abandoned him. Where was God? What kind of God would let this happen to such a faithful servant? Jesus on the cross cried out the opening line of Psalm 22, "My God, My God, why have you forsaken me?' expressing what one suspects is a real experience of the absence of God in the midst of suffering. If Jesus indeed had a last temptation, I suspect that its direction lay here, in the invitation to despair of the faithfulness of *Abba*. Yet he persisted in calling out to God, and this psalm does end on a note of hope that God will deliver the one who is suffering. Not withstanding this, in its own context the cross itself was not a holy event, as we think of the sacred in our stereotypical way. It was a civil execution; it was gruesome. Charged with a political crime, that of being king of the Jews, or a messianic pretender, Jesus died perceived by others to be wrong. He was one more troublesome upstart, dead between two others who were thieves. Nothing sacred about that. The depth of the sin of this world is reflected there on the cross.

Very early on, believers had the insight that after he died, Jesus descended into hell; we still confess this in the Creed. What does this mean? Jesus has gone down into the realm of the dead, to *Sheol*, the kingdom of shadows. What this symbolic way of speaking signifies is that even those who die victimized, those who disappear, those who are no longer part of the living history of the earth, those no longer remembered—all these people are not beyond the reach of the living God. The crucified Jesus has joined them, identifying with them, and bringing the power of the reign of God even there.

Resurrection

The story does not end here. Early in the morning two days later Mary Magdalene and other women disciples went to the tomb with oils for a last anointing of Jesus' body. Instead of a corpse they encountered the living Christ and bore witness of this to the other disciples. As events raced on the conviction of faith rose up: The raising of the dead which was supposed to happen on the last day with the coming of the reign of God has already begun to happen. By the loving power of God Jesus is transformed into glory, he is raised up.

Such existence is beyond our imagination, for it is life in another dimension beyond the limits of time and space; it is life in the dimension of God. It is better symbolized in the Easter Vigil liturgy, with its dramatic scenes of light out of darkness, proclamation of the creation story, sprinkling the water of new life, and sharing the eucharistic bread. Rather than coming to nothing in death, Jesus died into God. He is risen, whole and entire, as the embodied person he was in this life—his wounds are a sign of that.

If Jesus Christ is not risen, then our faith is in vain, and of all people we are stupid and most to be pitied (1 Cor 15:17–19). Everything depends upon this! First of all, God is revealed as really being the way that Jesus has preached. God is *Abba*, on the side of the one rejected, able to give a future to someone who has none. Henceforth, we can trust God to have the last word on our behalf, as indeed God had the first, and that word is *life*. In addition, the resurrection vindicates Jesus' message, ministry, even his person. He has been found guilty by human judges, who did away with him as a danger to religious tradition and the stability of the state. God now overturns the judgment of those judges and says there is another, divine judgment to be made about this crucified criminal, namely, that he is the Son of God. Finally, a future of hopes opens up for every human being and for the whole of creation. If God has so raised Jesus, then that same future becomes a real possibility and hope for the rest of us. "A piece of this earth, real to the core, is now forever with God in glory" . . . and the final *shalom* has broken into this world not just as a possibility but as a real beginning.

The overriding consideration is a christology "from below" is that the resurrection happened not just to anyone but to the Crucified One. And Jesus was not crucified by accident but because of the kind of ministry he persisted in carrying out. Thus the ministry interprets the death as well as the resurrection, giving us a concrete picture of precisely who was vindicated in the resurrection. It is the Jesus of the ministry who was shown to be Son of God in power through the resurrection—and this is the one whom disciples follow.

CORRELATION WITH THE COMMUNITY OF DISCIPLES

Bringing the story of Jesus into critical correlation with the lives of believers today involves us not just with our private selves but with the whole church and the community of the whole world. As the early disciples, after the resurrection and the outpouring of the Holy Spirit, preached and witnessed to Jesus Christ, giving him names out of their cultural contexts, so too today. Disciples are still inspired by the power of the Holy Spirit and, guided by the tradition generated through the experiences of the early communities, should be engaged in active following, in writing the fifth gospel so to speak. There are three moments in a living christology done this way in response to what is given by God in the story of Jesus.

1. Telling the story.

As a community the such is a story-telling group of people, telling the story of Jesus as the story of God with us. The church does in fact tell this story: Parents tell it to their children, catechists tell it, preachers tell it. At every Eucharist we also tell it, first at the reading of the gospel, and then at the very heart of the eucharistic prayer when language slips into a narrative mode and recounts how "on the night before he died, he took bread . . ." The story of his self-giving is at the center of our praise and thanks to God. We are a story-telling people! Particularly effective in illuminating the power of the story is a tale told by Martin Buber.

A rabbi related the following: "My grandfather was paralyzed. One day he was asked to tell about something that happened with his teacher, the great Balshem. Then he told how this saintly Balshem used to leap about and dance while he was at his prayers. As he went on with the story my grandfather stood up: he was so carried away that he had to show how the master had done it and he started to caper about dancing. From that moment he was cured."

Says Buber, *that* is how stories should be told. We add, *that* is how the story of Jesus should be told, so we become what we are in the telling. It is a transformative telling. It is a telling that makes Jesus alive and present, transforming us into persons of love and witness.

2. Living the story.

The church is called to put its feet in the footsteps of Jesus and walk the way that he walked. If he is the Way, the Truth, and the Life then his way must be our way. If he stood for compassionate love then so should the church. If he reached out to the most marginal people, then according to changing circumstances, so should the church. In fact only if we are in solidarity with him, who is in solidarity with God, who is in solidarity with those who suffer, will any christology be credible, especially in this world which is crying out for justice. The overriding importance of praxis leads some theologians such as Schillebeeckx to question whether "Who do you say that I am" with its resulting theoretical speculation is in fact the best way to pose the christological question today. It may well be more fruitful for Jesus Christ to be asking today "How have you been committed to the reign of God?" and to let our answer to the question of his meaning be shaped by our action on behalf of justice. In other words, the church must be about the business of the reign of God in order for its thought about Jesus Christ to be true.

3. Theorizing about the story.

In the midst of telling the story and living the story, we also engage in the classical activity of theorizing about it, but here theologians tend to be more reticent than in the past. We cannot define, ultimately, the mystery of the person of Jesus, the mystery of the suffering of the cross, the mystery of the victorious love of God that breaks through in the midst of it all. We are dealing here with the very depth of our faith. We can make affirmations about Jesus but we cannot grasp him in our concepts. Suggests have been made for reformulating the insights of the early councils. Would it be possible to rephrase Chalcedon in the terminology of our day and say, Jesus is in total solidarity with God (divine nature); Jesus is in total solidarity with us (human nature); and both of these solidarities form who he is and constitutes his person (one person)? This is one of Schillebeeckx's proposals, and open to discussion. Again, could we express the idea that Jesus is the Word of God in a more contemporary idiom by saying that he is the parable of God? He did not just tell parables but he *is* the story that God is telling the world. Instead of giving Jesus more exalted titles, could we simply say that Jesus is God's great No to suffering and God's great Yes to laughter? He did not bring joy in a superficial way but by entering into suffering on the cross and triumphing over it in the resurrection. These are some of the theorizings that have come up in this narrative approach. To date this christology has been rich in images and weak in metaphysics. The interest has been no so much on philosophical analysis of Jesus' inner constitution as in practical fidelity to this history. As church we are called to tell the story of Jesus, recall his dangerous memory, walk in his footsteps and, in the power of the Spirit, struggle against the forces of death. These actions will shape a practical, living christology in our own time.

CHAPTER 3

FOLLOWING JESUS: DISCIPLESHIP TODAY

DONALD SENIOR

*Jesus announces in word and in action that the reign of God is
already breaking through, that God is drawing near with salvation for all, and that the response demanded of people to the
reign is to turn their lives around, repent and believer in the
Good News. This Jesus, who surprises us and seems outrageous
in his proclamation, calls us to metanoia, that is, to conversion
and acceptance of the reign of God.*

*Jesus invited those who heard his message into a community of
disciples who traveled with him—listening, learning, knowing,
loving, watching, and then being sent forth on a mission to become the first witnesses to the presence of the reign of God in
Jesus and the first to tell the story of Jesus to others.*

—The Challenge of Catholic Youth Evangelization

PART ONE: WHAT IS DISCIPLESHIP?

A key biblical idea is that of "discipleship." It is one of the New
Testament's most powerful motifs. In this chapter I would like to spell out,
in more detail, some of its meaning.

Jesus gathered his first followers into a community of disciples. The Greek term for "disciple" (*matheteus*) means literally a "learner" or "student." Discipleship was a common mode of education in the ancient world. The Greek philosophers gathered disciples who followed their masters and learned wisdom from them. So, too, did students eager to learn the meaning of the Jewish law and searching for the compassion and prudence needed to interpret it well seek out rabbis or teachers. The Bible has always known famous "teacher-disciple" relationships such as that of Moses and Aaron, or Elijah and Elisha.

This form of personalized education or mentoring takes on particular importance as presented in the Gospels. The disciples that Jesus gathers and forms into a fragile community represent not only those historical figures who followed the teacher from Nazareth but, for the Christian reading of the Gospels, the disciples reflect the hopes and difficulties of Christians in every age. Discipleship becomes a metaphor for describing our whole relationship with Christ as a community of believers. Discipleship is not a temporary stage for Christians, with graduation moving us on to professional rank. We are always "learners" in the school of faith, constantly plumbing the depth of our relationship with Christ, constantly stumbling along the mysterious journey of faith. All of us, lay, religious, clergy, are beginners in the school of Jesus. It is important, therefore, to carefully review the meaning of discipleship as portrayed in the Gospels. There are five elements in the Gospel portrayal of discipleship that I would like to highlight. The first encounter of Jesus with his disciples, found in Mark 1:16–20, provides an excellent starting point for our reflections.

> As he passed by the Sea of Galilee, Jesus saw Simon and his brother Andrew casting their nets into the sea; they were fishermen. Jesus said to them, "Come after me, I will make you fishers of people." Then they left their nets and followed him. He walked along a little farther and saw James, the son of Zebedee, and his brother John. They too were in a boat mending their nets. Then he called them. So they left their father Zebedee in the boat along with the hired men and followed him.

A PERSONAL CALL

This Gospel story makes it clear that being a disciple of Jesus is not a career choice. It is a personal call. As in the case of the fishermen of Galilee, it can come unexpectedly into our lives and completely disrupt what we normally do. For others it can be a more gradual process, a slow awakening to the meaning of the Gospel for our lives. In every instance the call to follow Jesus is a gift of God, a "grace" in the full sense of the term. It is meant to reach down into the very depths of our being and affect every aspect of our life.

When we are called by someone we can either fall silent and turn away, or we can respond. The personal categories of call and response are important when considering the implications of Christian discipleship. Following Jesus does not entail only one aspect of our life; being a disciple touches everything about us—our values, our choices, our resources, our dreams. Therefore, we can expect changes and challenges once the call to be a disciple of Jesus has been heard and if we choose to respond to it.

A CALL TO FOLLOW JESUS

The Catholic bishops of the United States have declared: "Discipleship involves imitating the pattern of Jesus' life by openness to God's will in the service of others" (*Economic Pastoral* #47). This gets at the heart of the matter. The intrinsic meaning of discipleship is the notion of "following"; the disciple shapes his or her life on that of the master or mentor. "Follow me"—those two words from the Gospel story above distill the essence of Christian life.

Obviously "following" or "imitating" Jesus does not mean simply copying the surface details of his life, such as wearing first century garb or becoming an itinerant preacher. Imitating Jesus means that Christians are to shape their own lives in the pattern of Jesus. This is no simple process nor is there only one way of expressing the pattern of Christ's life in our own. Here is where the authentic disciple becomes a true learner by constantly reflecting on the teaching and example of Jesus and by trying to see their meaning in our everyday lives.

Jesus announced the nearness of God's reign in which the gifts of creation are not exploited but reverenced and shared, where human beings are treated as children of God, where oppression and injustice are expunged, where the sick are healed, where the disabled are not excluded but have full access to the community, where those pushed to the margins are drawn into the heart of the community, where enmity and violence are replaced by reconciliation and love. The Gospels illustrate that the reign of God was not some romantic utopian ideal for Jesus or beautiful words spoken without cost but rather something he embodied in his own life and mission. "What Jesus proclaims by word, he enacts in his ministry" (*Economic Pastoral* #42).

Each of the evangelists portrays a Jesus consumed with compassion, a tireless healer who was willing to break social and religious taboos to carry out his mission. The sick and dispossessed were drawn to him like a magnet and several times the Gospels describe compelling scenes as scores of the sick stream toward Jesus seeking to be healed. Jesus was not afraid to risk his own reputation—and ultimately his own safety—in order to affirm the dignity of the marginalized and to draw them into the center of his community. He invited the hated tax collector Levi to be a disciple and welcomed the bold affection of a public sinner in Simon's house. The detested Samaritans become the heroes of his stories. He included women among his disciples in an age and culture when women had no public status. Nor did Jesus fear to meet and even praise Gentiles who were regarded as enemies of his people.

In what he said and what he did Jesus embodied the values of God's Reign. "Following Jesus" means absorbing that same inclusive, compassionate, and just vision of the human family. It would surely be empty religious rhetoric if the ministry of Jesus were construed solely in private, personal terms. Following the will of Jesus, without fail, leads to the hard realities of social, economic, and political justice. It ultimately involves the Christian in political debate and public process.

Consider the Gospel of Luke. Jesus is portrayed as a prophet who challenges the community of Israel, particularly the rich and powerful, to remember their covenant with God, a covenant calling for the sharing of resources with the poor and defenseless. Like the great prophets before him, Jesus' challenge was disturbing and met fierce, death-dealing opposition. Jesus' death on the cross is the ultimate sign of his message: a life poured out in love for others. It is also the sign that looms ahead in every disciple's journey: following Jesus is not without cost. The way of discipleship can become the way of the cross.

A CHANGE OF HEART

The compelling beauty of the reign of God and the challenge it poses for many of our values and assumptions lead to another crucial dimension of discipleship. We are told that the disciples left everything—family members, hired hands, home, boats, livelihood—and followed Jesus. Jesus himself declared, "The reign of God is at hand! Reform your lives and believe in the Gospel" (Mk 1:15). The Gospel assumes that becoming a disciple of Jesus and attempting to live by the values of God's reign will mean changes in the way we think and act. It will mean "repentance." The Greek term used for this in the Gospel is *metanoia*. Literally it means a "change of mind" or "change of perspective." That is an apt description of what has to happen if the Gospel is to take root in our lives. We need to change our perspective. Not "perspective" in a superficial sense but a change in our entire view of things, looking at reality through the values and vision of human life expressed in the Gospel.

A COMMUNITY OF DISCIPLES

The story of Jesus' meeting with the disciples along the shore of Galilee reflects another profound assumption about biblical discipleship. To be a disciple means life with a community. Jesus' first disciples were called as a group and would be sent on missions in groups.

Unlike modern culture which prizes individualism, the biblical world gave first emphasis to the community—whether the family or the clan or the entire nation. The individual's worth and purpose had to be worked out with a community context. The value of individual dignity and rights treasured in our culture is also legitimate but it does not prepare us as well to deal with social and economic realities which are profoundly communitarian in nature. Catholic social teaching gives strong emphasis to the common good, and here it captures a key biblical virtue.

Jesus was embued with this sense of community, of the profound interrelationships of people with each other and with God. This, of course, was part of the rich heritage of Judaism upon which Jesus drew. The people of Israel were bound with God and with each other through the covenant. The Jewish law expressed the reality of that covenant and demanded an acute sense of justice and responsibility, especially for the poor and defenseless. The dominant symbol Jesus used to describe his mission, the "reign of God," is a social and political symbol and is essentially communal in nature. Jesus himself did not work as some sort of Lone Ranger. He gathered a community of disciples with whom he lived and taught and worked. His stories and teachings points to a restored community of Israel with lost sheep returned to the fold, alienated children brought back home, and people dealing with each other out of respect and truthfulness rather than out of lust or dishonesty.

This gives us a way of looking at the Church itself. John Paul II describes the church as "a community of disciples." Each member of the church is called to join with others in living out the Gospel. This sense of community is a Gospel value with tremendous importance for the future of the world. Avid consumerism, which feeds only its own appetite, is directly counter to the way of Christian discipleship.

FISHING FOR PEOPLE: THE ESSENTIAL DISCIPLESHIP TASK

Following Jesus means sharing in his mission. In the story of the first calling of disciples that mission is picturesquely described as "fishing for people". The prophet Jeremiah (16:16) speaks forcefully of the Lord sending out fishermen to snare people for God in the coming day of judgment. The image is also used by Habakkuk (2:14–15), again in a context of struggle and judgment. The fishing image in these biblical passages is not that of a lazy, hazy day of summer fishing by the old pond, but the chaos and struggle of storm churned sea.

It is an apt metaphor for the ministry of Jesus to which the disciples are called. Jesus' mission involved life and death and he, too, was a gatherer of people. His teaching and healing brought new life but it also involved struggle and conflict. To be a follower of Jesus does not mean simply gazing on the beauty of the Lord but being willing to live by his values and taking up his cause, the cause of justice, peace, and human dignity.

Social issues are not peripheral to Christian life nor are they a mere option reserved for those with a taste for such issues. The first disciples were not mountain top contemplatives but working people, and the call to be a follower of Jesus reached them in the marketplace. It is there that the mission of establishing the reign of God is to take place. It is up to modern disciples of Jesus, drawing on the wisdom of the Scripture, the strength of our Catholic tradition, and the inventiveness of people of good will, to incarnate that biblical vision within the realities of life today.

PART TWO: WHAT ARE THE CHARACTERISTICS OF CHRISTIAN DISCIPLESHIP?

In the Gospel narratives the disciples are mirror images of the Christian. In the hopes and failures of these first followers of Jesus are sketched the essential qualities and experiences of all followers of the Risen Christ. We will now highlight some of the main characteristics of discipleship presented in the Gospels. Matthew, Mark, and Luke do not portray the disciples in homogenized form. Just as the unique circumstances and purpose of each Gospel lead to distinctive portrayals of Jesus, their presentations of the disciples have special tones and emphases unique to each evangelist.

In all, the dramatic proportions of the Gospel call stories give us a hint at the major elements of gospel discipleship. The *initiative* in the stories is all on the side of Jesus. The disciples are called by him without preparation or merit. The call is a call *to follow Jesus*. And discipleship means *empowerment for mission*. The disciples are not called to learn the art of interpreting the Law, as rabbinic disciples were. The Christian disciple is summoned "to catch people," to be involved in Jesus' own decisive mission of salvation. Ultimately, the Christian call demands *response*. Disciples must leave all and set out on the journey of faith. We can use these four categories to reflect on the qualities of Christian discipleship, and therefore Christian life.

CHRISTIAN LIFE IS A GIFT

The call stories in the Gospels make this point without elaboration. Jesus breaks into the ordinary circumstances of human life and summons a person to begin the journey of discipleship. Galilean fishermen are merely the first in a string of gospel characters whose lives are transformed by the magnetic presence of Jesus. Levi, the tax collector, is called away from his toll booth at Capernaum (Mark 2:13–14). The tormented demoniac of Gadara is rescued from his life among the tombs and sent out on the mission to the Decapolis (Mark 5:1–20). The blind beggar Bartimaeus of Jericho has his pleas for mercy and for sight answered and he leaves his pauper's cloak behind to follow Jesus to Jerusalem (Mark 10:46–52). The Twelve are drawn from the inner circle of followers and sent out on mission (Matthew 10:1–8). Women are liberated and drawn into Jesus' ministry (Luke 3:1–3).

In citing this roster of gospel characters we move beyond those explicitly designated as "disciples" in the Gospels. But the boundaries between "disciple," "apostle," and other types of followers of Jesus are not clearly spelled out in the Gospels. All these stories illustrate what the inaugural call stories so clearly imply: Christian life is an unmerited gift. Faith is a grace. The Gospels show little interest in the process by which someone might grope their way to the first experience of faith. Perhaps this is because the Gospels were written for believers, not as enticement for non-Christians seeking first conversion but for Christians hoping to deepen a call they have already received. Therefore, the call is presented without ambiguity or preparation in order to emphasize its essential character as an initiative of the Lord. The process side of the faith experience is given more attention in the description of how the disciples will eventually respond to this gift, as we shall discuss below.

CHRISTIAN LIFE MEANS FOLLOWING JESUS

This dimension of discipleship is so massively expressed in the Gospels and so essential to their conception of Christian life that it risks being overlooked. Christian life means following-after—a relationship to Jesus. In the Synoptic Gospels this is narrated on practically every page. The disciples have almost no life of their own apart from their relationship with Jesus. We have brief glimpses of their backgrounds as fishermen, tax collectors, beggars (the absence of "fully qualified" types is notable!). We have a brief scene in the home of Simon's mother-in-law (Mark 1:29–31), but there is no real biographical interest in the disciples other than their relationship to the Master. The entire focus is on their presence with Jesus in his mission of healing and teaching and, eventually, in their reaction to Jesus and his mission.

The disciples become privileged witnesses to Jesus' awesome kingdom ministry. As he wades into the pain and confusion of Galilee, the disciples are there to observe the impact. On several occasions, select ones among their group are singled out to be present at such monumental displays as his raising of the daughter of Jairus or his transfiguration on the mountain. It is the disciples alone, bobbing helplessly at sea, who witness the great nature miracles of the calming of the storm and the walking on the water

—events that eloquently display Jesus' divine power over the chaos of the elements. Mark's Gospel, in particular, stresses that the disciples are the beneficiaries of Jesus' private instructions. On more than one occasion their teacher dismisses the crowds to concentrate his explanations on the disciples (4:10; 7:17; 10:23). The disciples, too, are taught to pray by Jesus (Luke 11:1–4). When they are under attack by opponents he rises to their defense (Matthew 9:14).

There is little, if anything, of Jesus' life that is not shared with the disciples. They are his constant companions. The Gospels clearly intend to make a statement about Christian life in portraying this bond between Jesus and disciple. To be with him, to learn from him, is not merely a passing phase in their initiation. It is the *goal* of Christian life. The Gospels ingeniously communicate this by sketching the life of discipleship as essentially a *following* of Jesus. There is no point in the narrative at which the disciple graduates into the status of master. They are always "on the road," following behind their Lord.

Mark probably deserves the credit for being the first to cast the experience of Christian life into the journey metaphor. The dizzying round of healing and teaching that characterizes Jesus' mission in Galilee in the early chapters of Mark gives way to a single-minded journey to Jerusalem. Jesus begins to speak openly of his impending death (Mark 8:31–32) and his disciples, hardly comprehending, find themselves drawn into that fateful journey with their Master. The journey to cross and eventual victory dominates the middle parts of the narrative in the Gospels of Mark, Matthew, and Luke. Mark 10:32 captures in a single frame the demanding reality of Christian discipleship. Jesus is on the way to Jerusalem, to the complete giving of his life in service, while the dumbfounded and fearful disciples follow along behind him. Essentially the same pattern is adapted by Matthew. Luke seems to develop it even more. In 9:51 Jesus sets his face toward Jerusalem and begins the exodus that will carry him to death and final glory. The journey of the disciples will bring them not only to Jerusalem, but under the impulse of the Spirit, will thrust them out into the world as witnesses to the Risen Christ, a continuing journey of discipleship narrated in Acts.

There is, in effect, no real collegiality in the community of Jesus. The figure of Jesus dominates. He remains elusively "out in front," drawing the disciples beyond themselves and their accustomed way of life. Even their relationships with each other remain in dependence on *his* presence. When Jesus is taken away, the bonds break apart in flight and panic. Only when he comes back to them in the triumph of resurrection are the bonds renewed and solidified.

There is little need to moralize on these Gospel images. The metaphors of "following" and "journeying with" Jesus have nourished Christian spirituality from the first century to the present day. The images are, of course, subject to much elaboration. Their central statement is clear. Christian life is not an ideology or an ascetical technique or a set of moral instructions. Its essential character is a faith relationship with the person of Jesus Christ. Everything else is secondary to and a consequence of that bond.

CHRISTIAN LIFE AS EMPOWERMENT FOR MISSION

The Gospels assert, without qualification, that the presence of Jesus effects transformation. To encounter him is to be changed, one way or the other. The tide of broken humanity that flows toward him is made whole: the blind see, the lame walk, those tormented by evil are liberated, the ignorant are instructed, the hungry fed, the dead are given life. People also react with hostility and reject him. There are few, if any, casual observers who confront the Jesus of the Gospels and walk away coolly unaffected.

By these stories the evangelists define the mission of Jesus. In the Synoptic Gospels the dominating metaphor is that of the coming reign of God. The person and ministry of Jesus brings to Israel the first taste of God's definitive rule, the longed-for reign that would break the bonds of oppression and pain, and realize humanity's dream of freedom and fulfillment.

The Synoptic Gospels present the disciples as having a stake in this mission of Jesus. They are called not only to be formed and instructed by Jesus but to share in his mission. They, like Jesus, are "to catch people alive." That intriguing image—"fishers of people"—seems to echo images of judgment in the Hebrew scriptures, as in Jeremiah 16:16; where the prophet speaks of the final day when God would hook and pull people ashore. Jesus' mission is captured in this same fierce imagery. Redemption is a labor, a brawling struggling with the power of evil, a mission which is, literally, a matter of life and death for humanity.

The disciples are bonded with Jesus in order to be empowered for this same redemptive mission. In a multitude of ways the Gospels make this clear. The apostles (literally, "ones sent") are called and named to go on mission. Their marching orders duplicate the transforming acts of Jesus' own ministry: announcing the advent of the Kingdom, healing, casting out evil, teaching (Mark 3:13–19; Matthew 10:1–8; Luke 9:1–6). They are destined to be the founders of the ideal Israel, the "Twelve" who will realize Israel's dream of peace and life without tears (Luke 22:28–30). The mission instructions do not minimize the cost of such a mission. Like their mentor, the disciples must travel light, expect an atmosphere of crisis, be ready to suffer rejection and persecution (Matthew 10:9–42). The mission is a constitutive part of the Christian experience. The transforming words and actions of Jesus are to be carried out by his followers. That is why the Gospel story is told.

CHRISTIAN LIFE IS A SPIRITED RESPONSE

The inaugural call stories in the Gospels add one other element to the portrayal of Christian discipleship. The invitation to follow Jesus and to share in his mission demands total response. Without a moment of hesitation the Galilean fishermen leave their old life behind and follow Jesus. Fortunately for the Christian reader, the rest of the Gospel story shatters this idealized picture. Here, in fact, is one of the most enticing aspects of the Gospel literature. The evangelists refuse to idealize the founding members of the Christian community. The picture is, of course, not entirely negative. The disciples are the inner circle. They are the ones called to be with Jesus and the ones to whom he will entrust his mission. As the Gospel narratives progress, the disciples do, in fact, participate in Jesus' ministry and come to recognize him as the Christ. But these positive affirmations coexist with stunning glimpses into the disciple's obtuseness and failure.

The evangelist Mark emphasizes this side of the picture best. The Markan disciples seem to stumble through the Gospel story: baffled by Jesus' parables (4:13), perplexed at his teaching (7:18), their senses completely dulled to the meaning of his person and mission (6:51–52; 8:14–21). Their failure is not confined to benign ignorance. As the story develops their lack of comprehension takes an ugly turn. When Jesus begins to speak of the cross, and of the necessity of giving one's life in order to save it, Peter rudely attempts to stifle Jesus (8:32). Other disciples argue among themselves about who is the greatest person, or seek after positions of power, while Jesus tries to instruct them on the necessity of service (9:34; 10:37). These and many other examples in Mark prepare us for the stark failure of the disciples at the climax of Jesus' mission. When the moment of the Passion comes, Judas betrays Jesus. Peter denies him. All the rest flee in panic.

The other evangelists tone down Mark's negative portrayal. Matthew, for example, prefers the label "little faith," where Mark would bluntly say the disciples have "no faith" (compare Matthew 8:26 with Mark 4:40). Because Luke wants to emphasize the crucial role of continuity between Jesus and the church played by the twelve apostles, he soft-pedals their failures in the Passion story. (In Luke, for instance, there is no mention of the disciples' flight at the moment of Jesus' arrest.) He notes the efficacy of Jesus' prayer for the perseverance of the Twelve (22:31–32). But neither Matthew nor Luke chose to omit the chilling fact that Jesus was betrayed by one apostle and denied by another.

Why are these stories of abject failure included in the Gospels? Here, I believe, is where the Gospel writers and their communities dealt with the real cost of discipleship and the process of life-long conversion. Faithful love and active service—essential symptoms of Christian commitment—are deep human aspirations and universally admired. But for them to take hold and become the determining principles of human decision means a break with the *actual* value systems of our culture. It means a profound social and personal transformation that only the power of grace can effect. Put in the graphic metaphors of the Gospel narratives, Christian discipleship is not accomplished in the quickly peaking joy of the initial call by the lakeside. Its story winds hesitantly along the road and on the churning sea; its moments come in glimpses, between confusion, bafflement and plain failure.

From one angle, the wart-laden portraits of the disciples in the Gospels might seem crude and unforgiving. But the tone is ultimately one of compassion. In spite of the most abject failure and apostasy, the invitation for reconciliation remains open. Mark ends his story with the discovery of the empty tomb and with the message that Jesus' scattered disciples will see him again in Galilee (16:7). Matthew gathers the shattered community of Jesus on a mountain top and has the Risen Christ send them into the world as his apostles (28:16–20). Luke has the Risen Jesus retrieve the disillusioned disciples of Emmaus and send them back to an ecstatic gathering in Jerusalem where the same reconciling Lord has already left his mark (24:1–35).

The image of the Church that seeps through these narratives is not that of a sterile moral elite, but of a very human community able to have compassion for weakness without despairing of its call to greatness. The story of the disciples is the Church's story. It is told with disarming simplicity, but it carries the power of instruction and challenge for every believer who has felt the tug of the call.

CHAPTER 4

THE SPIRITUAL HUNGERS OF AMERICA'S YOUTH

REYNOLDS R. EKSTROM

Throughout history, the church has been entrusted with pro-claiming the story of Jesus, living the Good News, responding to the needs and hungers of the human family, and celebrating this relationship with Jesus in worship. In a multitude of ages, cultures and settings, the reign of God continues to break through, affirming the diversity through which God speaks. To-day the reign of God is breaking through in the cultural experi-ences of young people, and the church is challenged to proclaim that breakthrough and to bring the Gospel of Jesus into dia-logue with their story.

The world today, as in Jesus' day and on through history, some-times seems dominated by the clear effects of a broken relation-ship with God: war, oppression, poverty, racism, sexism, mate-rialism, and hopelessness. In recognizing such personal and social sin, we begin to realize that, indeed, today's world is as much in need of salvation as it was in Jesus' time. Within this context, young people yearn for a sense of hope and fulfillment in their individual lives.

Young people hunger for healing in their personal, individual lives, as well as in their relationships, families and communities. A full understanding of the salvation offered by Jesus speaks to all of these dimensions. The Christian conviction is that Jesus and his message free us from sin, bind us in love, and call us to fullness in God both as individuals and as a community. In the church's ministry among young people today, our response to this call to love must be grounded in the acknowledgment of the hungers of today's adolescents.

—The Challenge of Catholic Youth Evangelization

THE OTHER DAY A QUESTION I OFTEN HEAR, in one way or another, came up again in conversation. What are the spiritual needs of young people today? This is not a question I take lightly. In doing some reading about it, later that night, I was struck by the truth of the following quote:

When children are the topic of adult conversation nowadays, they are sometimes portrayed in less than complimentary images. Children, some say, have lost any sense of right and wrong, and as such are given to drugs, sexual promiscuity, and the empty hedonism of popular music. Children have also lost any respect for the authority of their parents and of the adult world in general. Moreover, they are sometimes thought to have little sense of care and concern for others and therefore little or no sense of the public duty that comes with responsible citizenship (*Girl Scouts* 101).

The piece I was reading suggested that such portrayals of young people today are ill-considered. They underestimate contemporary youth's ability to confront and deal with moral and spiritual issues. They are, ultimately, stereotypes ("bland generalities" about all children today) which do severe "injustice to the real diversity" which exists among young people, adolescents in particular, in our day.

The conversation, earlier in the day, had not stooped to labeling, teen-bashing, and name-calling. Participants, myself included, had genuinely tried to name those things which adolescents spiritually crave. We had concluded, tentatively, that it is oh-so risky to generalize about youth in the 1990s. We had begun to identify that adolescents do not inhabit some ghetto of their own, to use Robert Coles' phrase. In fact, we had echoed something which Coles has said emphatically, based upon his observation of many young people, unhealthy and seriously troubled youngsters alike,

> No small number of . . . young people have become what they are because they have lived in a certain kind of *adult* world where they have known abuse, addiction, bursts of temper, abandonment—the psychological litany goes on (Coles 73).

Of course, our conversation had eventually gotten around to the topic of adults. It always does in such situations. We spoke of how caring, Christian witnesses and caring, Christian support structures (like family households, adult friends, positive peer influences, welcoming ministry gathering spots, and so on) will make a difference in the lives of youths we know—if only we find the right combination of these and the right formula for making such things possible. If only this . . . If only that, kids would finally, miraculously, achieve that sweet-spot, devoutly wished, which ushers in spiritual well-being.

I often try to find a real-life story or two which testify to percentages found in studies. I often try to locate concrete persons who embody what conversation's opinions only suggest. Statistic to story. Opinion to experience. That daytime conversation had triggered many memories. So, as I read the measured thoughts of many expert researchers, on the subject of how to reach out and help young people today, I began to look homeward. From the mean streets of inner cities and the hidden households of rural America—described so well on the pages of statistics and studies—I slowly stepped back onto my own home turf, and began to discover sacred ground.

WELCOME TO MY NEIGHBORHOOD

We live in a complex of townhouses in a suburban setting not too far from downtown New Orleans. There are many different types of children, adolescents, and households within a block or two of our place. As I look out our front windows, to the right or to the left, there are situations and ministry-related challenges which, probably, could not have even been imagined just several decades ago.

Down the sidewalk, to the right, you and I will find Spencer and Thomas. Spencer is African-American, about 14, and stretching into a maturing adolescent frame. He lives with his parents but seems to spend lots of time alone—particularly during summer days and on days whenever school is out. Thomas is a younger boy, maybe 11 or 12 now, and scrawny at best. He lives with his mother, around the bend in the street. Thomas would love to get into the neighborhood ball games, but he hangs back because he is so small and so unskilled when it comes to sports. Spencer likes to join the pickup football games but otherwise doesn't participate. Both have eyes that seem to light up when an adult speaks to them. However, Thomas seems to studiously avoid contact with adult males if he can.

Occasionally, Spencer can be seen hanging with Jeff, especially on those days when there is almost nothing else to do. Jeff is likewise African-American and carries a trouble-maker label in our area. He lives with his grandfather, a man who believes Jeff can do no wrong. Jeff's father, we have heard, is in prison and there is no word about a mother.

Also, to our right, is Cheryl's household. Cheryl has a daughter about five years old. She doesn't know her natural father. Cheryl, a professional woman, got pregnant intentionally in order to have her own child. Her daughter seems pretty happy. She zooms her tricycle up and down the sidewalk. She says hello to just about everybody who wanders by. Cheryl got married about six months ago, just after she had given birth to a son, Taylor. Her husband, Tony, has now left the scene—officially speaking, they have separated. We will probably never seem him around again. The rumor is that this is a relationship pattern of his. This makes me sad for Cheryl's two kids but even sadder for a cute but troubled kid on our left named Alicia.

To the left of our household, six steps up the sidewalk, lives Alicia, Katie and sometimes Woody. Katie is the mother, Alicia is the eight-year-old daughter, and Woody is the new boyfriend. Of course, Katie and Tony were married when they first moved into the neighborhood. Alicia is his child. When Katie and Tony decided to split, he moved in with Cheryl, immediately, only three doors away. Katie has had to force him to pay child support through the legal system. Before Tony silently moved away, Alicia had not spent any time with her father for several months. She is bright, friendly, and curious about things. Yet, she also seems very lonely, confused, and even haunted at times. Now, she spends lots of time with her two dogs. Now and then, she asks me to play ball with her.

Justin is 16. This past summer, he was Alicia's baby-sitter during daytimes while Katie and Woody were away at work. Justin lives next to them with his father, Jim, and stepmother, Joanne. They all seem nice enough but there has been lots of trouble. Justin's mother fled to France after her divorce from Jim. Justin hardly ever hears from her. He has been hospitalized, several times, at a place that treats psychologically troubled adolescents. Justin struggles with school work. There were many rumors, for months, that he alone was responsible for acts of vandalism (which have largely stopped) around the complex. He goes out of his way, day after day, to talk to me and to any other adult who will spend a few minutes with him—as does Alicia, by the way. Both kids always seem hungry for attention, any kind of attention.

Beside Justin's house are three recently vacated townhomes. Each housed children up to two months ago. Gerald, a 12-year-old, lived with his mother and older half-brother. His mother and half-brother are black. Gerald is part black, part Hispanic. He was always a nice enough kid—very quiet and polite—but usually he seemed very lonely. His mother worked two jobs to keep them afloat. Their little family was forced to move quite quickly because they rented their place and the landlord suddenly needed it. Brad was a deeply troubled 13-year-old when he left the area. Brad's family occupied the unit next to Gerald's. He lived with his mother, her boyfriend, and two older sisters who kept a steady stream of boyfriends moving in and out of the household, literally, twenty-four hours a day. Brad showed signs of sociopathic behavior that scared many kids and adults around the complex. The family departed quickly after several instances of physical threats and property damage nearby. Bradley was a 15-year-old who lived next to "bad Brad," as several neighbors unkindly referred to him. His father, Joaquin, and mother, Connie, were very congenial. They always had time to talk or to help a neighbor in need. Two months ago, they moved out rapidly, under the cover of darkness, and have not been heard from since. Our condo association had noticed that the parents were not paying their dues and demanded that they do so. When I think about Alicia, the two Brads, Gerald, and the others, the word uprooted keeps coming to mind. I often wonder what comes next for each of them.

NO TIME LIKE THE PRESENT

Unprecedented situations, unprecedented challenges. These are the kinds of phrases that researchers and helping professionals seem to use, frequently, to describe the mysteries and the ironies which shape adolescents' lives in your neighborhood and mine these days. In commenting recently on the spiritual life of young Americans, the George H. Gallup International Institute noted:

Young Americans face unprecedented challenges—diminishing economic opportunities, changing gender roles, the lure of self-fulfillment as an ultimate personal goal, and a spiritual and ethical environment pervaded by cultural and religious relativism, to name a few. At the same time, young people find they have fewer personal and institutional resources upon which to draw. Family networks are weaker. Diminishing government resources are pulling the floor from beneath the urban young who are the most disadvantaged. What role are religious institutions playing in the lives of young people? (Gallup 8).

Since, generally speaking, we have never known a time quite like the present, I believe it is important to answer questions such as, "What are the spiritual needs of young people today?" and "What should religious institutions do to help?" in two ways. On the personal level, I must ask how am I responding to and acting on behalf of the Alicias, Justins, and Geralds who inhabit my neighborhood and cruise daily through the local shopping malls. On institutional (church or school) levels, we must choose to get busy with concerned others who are willing to answer questions such as "What can and should we do now?" In both cases, it helps to have as complete a sketch of the as-yet uncharted turf of adolescent experience, in the '90s, as is possible.

By the dawn of the 1990s, there were about 24 million teenagers in the United States. They constituted, therefore, about 9% of the general population. Twenty-six percent of them were either African-American or members of other racial groups. Seventy-four percent of them were white. About fifteen years from now, in the year 2010, teenagers will represent only 7.5 percent of the U.S. population. Thirty-four percent will be either black or members of another minority group. Sixty-six percent will be white. As always, both today and tomorrow, it will remain risky to generalize about them because they are products of varied cultural, familial, and moral influences. As George Gallup has put it,

We increasingly are becoming a nation of diverse racial backgrounds. Nowhere is this better seen than in our largest urban areas where children of color are becoming the majority, not a minority . . . non-white young people, if anything, are more religiously inclined than are many who are white. Past generations in the melting pot of America struggled to understand the different traditions of Protestants, Catholics, and Jews. Now, to these faiths, are added Muslims, Buddhists, and other faiths from

Africa and Asia. Interfaith understanding, especially for our youth, must assume new responsibilities (Gallup 15–16).

Generally, certain values and virtues were held in high regard by high school seniors in the States in the later '80s. Financial and occupational values, which are future-oriented, were on the rise. Values related to compassion and self-restraint were decreasing in importance. Search Institute reported the following in 1986 (Search 13).

Values of American High School Seniors	*Percentage Saying Value is Important*
Success in my line of work	61
Giving my children better opportunities than I've had	59
Having lots of money	23
Making a contribution to society	17
Working to correct social and economic problems	9

How American Adolescents View Work	*1976*	*1979*	*1983*
Is a job which gives you a chance to earn a great deal of money very important to you?	48	54	56
Is a job with high status and prestige very important to you?	22	26	28
Is a job that directly helps people very important to you?	53	49	48

Reflection on these emerging data calls to mind a point made by the seminal, sociological commentary *Habits of the Heart*. In that study, Robert Bellah and colleagues insisted that to find the true meaning of human existence one must somehow abandon individualistic goals and pursue, instead, a life course through which one lives for the common (social) good (Bellah 1985). With few empirical statistics but many personal observations and stories to go on, we might be able to say we live in a time in which many, many adolescents in the United States are not developing as strong a commitment to the common good as we would wish (Search 12-14).

On the whole, many things seem to be worrisome to American adolescents. The respected *Journal of Home Economics*, at the University of Michigan, recently reported findings on ten key causes for concern typical among the young these days:

- Having a good marriage and family life
- Choose a career/finding steady work
- Doing well in school
- Being successful
- Having strong friendships
- Paying for college
- The country going downhill
- Making a lot of money
- Finding the purpose of life
- Contracting AIDS (Gelman 16)

For years, though, psychologists have been commenting forcefully that the underlying, worrisome syndrome cutting through all adolescents' experiences and worries today is adult-strength pressure or stress. Other commentators, along with these psychologists, add a reminder. The concerns of youth, spiritual and otherwise, as perceived by adults are often not the actual, stress-induced concerns we hear about when we listen to the actual voices of contemporary children. For example,

> "crisis" youth problems ranked low as a major concern for children—teenage pregnancy (5%), suicide (3%), violence in schools (2%), and alcohol abuse (1%). The pressure to engage in these activities was also listed low compared to other concerns—38% felt pressure to "fit in;" 23% of junior and senior high schools feel pressure to have sex, only 16% to drink alcohol, only 6% felt pressure to take drugs, and only 5% to join a neighborhood gang (*Girl Scouts* xvi).

Fundamentally, the greatest worries and pressures children now face have to do with fulfilling expectations of the adult world.

> The social expectations creating pressure are (1) obedience to parents and teachers (80%), getting good grades (78%), (3) preparing for the future (69%), and (4) earning money (62%). When asked about the one problem they worry about most for themselves, they answered "the pressure to do well in school and sports" (24%) and "what to do with your life" (17%) (*Girl Scouts* xvi).

In the shady nooks of our tentative, emerging, and colorful portrait of youth in American society in the '90s—one brush-stroked by many stereotypes, scary small talks, stunning statistical references, stories upon stories, and stressful change for almost all persons—we find traditional Christian churches. In general, do churches today help or hinder adolescents in their spiritual quest? Some help, of course, and some hinder. Americans of all ages identify religion as a very significant influence in their lives. Those who draw meaning from their religious beliefs are, nowadays, far more likely than others to experience such spiritual uplifts as closeness to family members, a sense of self-fulfillment, and enthusiasm about the future. However, recent research cautions us with regard to religion and the young.

> At this time, thousands of young people, who view their own churches or faith communities as sterile and spiritually unrewarding, are joining the ranks of the unchurched or are opting for the nearest fad religion or self-proclaimed messiah (Gallup 8).

One telling sign of the times, culled from contemporary research, is that the lives of adult baptized Christians today often do not differ much from the lifestyles of the non-baptized. Is it any wonder that idealistic, disillusioned adolescents and young adults wander away from such lukewarm Gospel witness.

Many adults in churches who try to authentically listen to the voices of today's young people, nevertheless, see much cause for hope, despite the apparent and unfortunate problems which have befallen contemporary youth, families, church structures, and other social institutions. These adults choose to view youth as a source of hope and human resource, not as harbingers of doom; as power and positive presence, not problems; as developments in progress, not demons of despair. Their vision underscores the critical need to address, especially through church agencies, the spiritual needs and hungers of adolescents in the '90s. And after all, the state of spiritual well-being among young people, today and tomorrow, will foretell the health and vitality of Christian life (and its local faith communities), in the United States, for the year 2000 and beyond.

There is no time like the present. Specifically, it is time to think about what people who represent Christian church communities, especially church-sponsored ministries, can do to better listen to the voices of youth today in order to satisfy youth's spiritual hungers. In other words, it is time to investigate what ministers who come from Christian communities can and must do to make adolescents' life stories more spiritually fertile than sterile. Practical steps will become more clear, in all likelihood, once the most basic needs—the fundamental spiritual hungers—of young people today are properly named (Gallup 17). Broadly speaking, they fall into a trio of foundational desires and these shake up our cultural misunderstandings and stereotypes. The three are: (1) a longing for meaningful relationships, (2) a longing to know what life is all about, and (3) an emerging drive to be of service to others.

ADOLESCENTS HUNGER FOR MEANINGFUL RELATIONSHIPS AND STRUCTURE

The document *The Challenge of Catholic Youth Evangelization* notes that young people "have a strong need for relationships, (and) for connecting with others on a variety of levels. It is within these connections that love and acceptance are experienced." Family households, peer groups, and individual relationships, ideally, should help meet this need. So should positive experiences in school, church, and wider society. A major challenge faced by those who do ministry among the young is to shape communities which emphasize acceptance, belonging, and unconditional friendship on behalf of the Gospel (*Challenge* 6).

Along these lines, some adolescents today are blessed indeed. In a guest editorial for *Newsweek* magazine, for example, Brad Wackerlin, recently graduated from high school, wrote:

> I write this article to show that a teenager can survive in today's society. Actually I'm doing quite well. I haven't fathered any children, I'm not addicted to any drugs, I've never worshipped Satan and I don't have a police record. I can even find Canada on a map along with its capital, Ottawa. I guess my family and friends have been supportive of me, for I've never been tempted to become one of those teenage runaways I'm always reading about. Call me a rebel but I've stayed in school and (can it be true?) I enjoyed it . . . My only goal in writing this is to point out the "bum rap" today's teenager faces. I feel the stereotypical teen is, in fact, a minority. The majority are teenagers who, day in and day out, prepare themselves for the future and work at becoming responsible adults (Wackerlin 22).

A body of contemporary polling data indicates that he is very right about several things. Yet a significant percentage of young people, nevertheless, struggle for a place in our society and are seriously at-risk, even as we now stare at Brad's words. Often adult perceptions about youths' lives fail to discern the little nuances which tell us, in meaningful ways, why some adolescents like Brad thrive and some slip into the deepest of human troubles. A subtle, numbing suspicion (a stereotype) seems to be somehow working its way into the psyches of many parents and other adults in our society. It whispers that kids today mostly are in fact sullen and self-absorbed. Secretive and rude. People of the closed door. Withdrawn and surly. Rebels in black clothing, as it were.

Ruby Takanishi, recent director of the Carnegie Council on Adolescent Development, says, "The society is still permeated by the notion that adolescents are different, that their hormones are raging around and they don't want to have anything to do with their parents or other adults." However, many adolescents somehow evolve into rather stable, thriving young adults—even some of the most at-risk and challenged adolescents. Francis Ianni, a professor of education and director of the Institute for Social Analysis, maintains that "a lot of people have attributed this to some inner resilience" or some secret invulnerability factor which adolescents have discovered. Actually, he says, "What we've seen in practically all cases" in which a young man or woman proceeds through adolescence into young adulthood in thriving shape "is some caring adult figure who was a constant in that kid's life" (Ianni 1989).

Despite our fondest wishes, many adolescents today spend lots of hours alone in their rooms. Many also share heavily in the spreading sense of isolation and disconnection prevalent in the young. Years ago, David Elkind explained some of the barriers we face, right now, in getting into contact with young people and offering them a sense of meaningful connection, relationship, and structure. In 1984, he said:

> There is no place for teenagers in American society today—not in our homes, not in our schools, and not in society at large. This was not always the case: barely a decade ago, teenagers had a clearly defined position in the social structure. They were the "next generation," the "future leaders" of America. Their intellectual, social, and moral development was considered important, and therefore it was protected and nurtured. . . Society recognized that the transition from childhood to adulthood was difficult and that young people needed time, support, and guid-

ance in this endeavor. In today's rapidly changing society, teenagers have lost their once privileged position. Instead, they have
had a premature adulthood thrust upon them . . . Perhaps the
best word to describe the predicament of today's teenagers is
"unplaced" . . . they are unplaced in the sense that there is no
place for a young person who needs a measured and controlled
introduction to adulthood . . . few adults are genuinely committed to helping teenagers attain a healthy adulthood. Young people
are thus denied the special recognition and protection that society previously accorded their age group. Young people today
are quite literally all grown up with no place to go (Elkind 3–5).

Put another way, by Marc Miringhoff for Fordham University's Index
of Social Health, "If you take the teens in the '50s—the "Ozzie and Harriet"
generation—those kids lived on a less complex planet. They could be kids
longer" (Gelman 12). Today it is more difficult than ever before for adolescents to build strong, integrated personal identities. They are quite vulnerable to stresses induced by the various choices, losses, at-risk experiences, and frustrations they often have forced upon them. Feeling disconnected, lonely, angry, yes, even sometimes betrayed by parents, teachers,
and others, they periodically withdraw into their private rooms, literal and
figurative. Even those adolescents who are "doing fine, against all odds,"
like Brad Wackerlin, and others who eagerly want to get on with their
lives, show signs of this behavior.

In recent years sociologists and youth ministers alike have begun to
realize anew that ironically youth remain more dependent on adults today
than was formerly believed. Americans on the whole, youth included, are
among the loneliest people in the world locked in the prisons of their own
hearts, as deTocqueville once observed. Pop culture is becoming increasingly impersonal and centered on individualistic pursuits. The hunger and
thirst for meaningful relationships and caring structures (small communities, in particular) in which Christian witnesses and models can be encountered, have only intensified for many young people in the last decade,
although these physical and emotional needs often go unvoiced or, even
worse, go unheard (as in overlooked, denied or shunned) by adults who
should have known better.

Recent research and the ministerial experiences of many have firmly
indicated that the "extended family—parents and close relatives—continues to be the most foundational influence in the lives of children."
However, key "adults in the (wider) community also play an important

role in the lives of children—particularly religious leaders, school counselors, and leaders of youth organizations" (*Girl Scouts* xv). As the Gallup Institute has noted lucidly, "At a time when many families, schools, and (other) communities seem incapable of providing moral guidance to young people, the church becomes the obvious choice to fill this vacuum through its youth activities and educational efforts" and other caring, relational means for reaching out to kids today, especially those who are "unchurched," "un-Gospeled," at risk, or among the deeply alienated and wandered-away. And, likewise, as studies have consistently shown, for adolescents increasingly influenced by single-parent and soon-to-be-divorced households "youth religious leaders can play a vital part in young people's lives by becoming the positive (adult) role models so many desperately need" (Gallup 15).

Only by incorporating some young people into caring, personal relationships and in developing supportive, structured programs which care for youth's real—not imagined—needs, will the youthful hunger for community and connection be marginally addressed. In such circumstances, other hopes, hungers, hurts, and adolescent questions can also be recognized and brought into the light of pastoral care (*Challenge* 12–13). In this way, adults—and adolescents who minister to peers—can become (and embody) the Good News of Christian community, not just talk about it.

ADOLESCENTS HUNGER FOR PEOPLE WHO WILL LISTEN TO THEM

The document *The Challenge of Catholic Youth Evangelization* stresses that adolescents "experience a fundamental need to feel worthwhile and important." It adds that

> This need is met when they experience the attention and interest of others, providing the basis for self-esteem and self-confidence. Young people need to be affirmed in their goodness and giftedness. They need to be appreciated and loved. They need to be listened to (*Challenge* 6).

As many as one-third of all Americans have a low sense of self-worth and impoverished self-images, but percentages are higher, typically, among adolescents. The combination of a sense of unplaced-ness, with the adult-style stresses it induces, and low self-esteem makes young people today vulner-able to social ills like alcohol or other substance abuse, criminal activities, dropping out of school, and sexual dabblings (Gallup 13). The failure of many parents and other adults to spend time with and pay personal attention to adolescents, simply because youth are worthwhile and valuable human persons, is tragic in many cases. Interestingly but sadly, some researchers indicate that actual time spent by adolescents with family members, in the U.S., decreases by 50% or more between the ages of 10 and 15. Many '90s adolescents never get strokes just for being who they are. Often, these days, if an adolescent gets a stroke or positive comment, of any sort, from an adult, it tends to be for "what" he or she can become (e.g., a doctor, a lawyer, a perfect student) rather than "who" he or she actually is.

David Elkind warned parents and adult caregivers about this in his book, *All Grown Up and No Place to Go*, in the most forceful of terms.

> We hurry young people as children, then unplace them as teen-agers. We cannot, dare not, persist on this dangerous course of denying young people the time, the support, and the guidance they need to arrive at an integrated definition of self . . . Their (spiritual need is real and pressing. We harm them and endanger the future of our society if we leave them, as our legacy, a patch-work sense of personal identity (Elkind 21).

Denying young people their right to be heard and appreciated can lead to resentments and feelings of depression. Robert Coles has shown us how combative today's adolescents, who wander through experiences unheard and resentful, can really sound. He quotes one as saying,

> "I get tired of reading about 'us' and 'them'—like the people who say they know what teenagers are like—the experts and the politicians and those people up in the pulpit saying we're no damn good. I wish they'd look at people their own age . . . All this sleaze today, look where it's coming from. The ones who will tell you about noisy teenagers and their music and their sex and their drugs—they're the ones you see in the papers, with all their lies and crimes being reported. There's a lot of hypocrites around" (Coles 71).

On the whole, then, we can and should know that adolescents want caring adults to listen to them, spend time with them, and pay attention to the things which they feel are worthy of attention. When they get little personal appreciation and recognition they face great dangers. A special report on them in *Time* recently noted, "If teenagers are to stop feeling irrelevant, they need to feel needed, both by the family and by the larger world" (Gelman 15-16). It is sad, as Ernest Boyer has noted poignantly, that youth often complain about feeling isolated and disconnected from the wider world at precisely the time many of them are deciding who they are and where they fit in the big picture of life.

The Search Institute, headquartered in Minneapolis, has developed a brief profile on the types of adults whom adolescents choose to be their best listeners. In 1987, Search reported that "an adult most likely to be consulted" by a youth experiencing some sort of trouble has three characteristics. First, he or she has a reputation for being nonjudgmental, caring, and supportive. Second, he or she is perceived by youth as available. And third, he or she shows to youth a willingness to take the time to really listen. As the Search commentary says, "There is a great scarcity nowadays of adults who are accessible (to adolescents) and who will nod affirmatively when a young person asks, 'Got a couple of minutes?'" (Search 22).

Is it too much to say that adolescents spiritually crave friends, particularly adult friends, who will spend time and lavish attention on them? The Search report, titled "Adolescents' Search for Trusted Friends," concluded that there are many self-esteem poor youth today who lack an adequate "support network" of listening, caring others.

> Many live in large cities, perhaps having moved to their neighborhood recently. They attend large, impersonal schools, and have no connection with any youth-serving organization. Though they may not themselves recognize it, this lack of adult support is a genuine (spiritual) deprivation, and one that society should seek to remedy (Search 22).

An interesting new study by George Gallup and Jim Castelli, called *The People's Religion*, says that the unchurched and the religiously dis-identified, in American mainstream society, say that one key thing which would lead them back today to active church attendance is "find(ing) a pastor, priest, or rabbi with whom I could share my religious needs and doubts" (Gallup and Castelli 1989). *The Challenge of Catholic Youth Evangelization* supports this line of thinking, but takes things several steps farther. It maintains that if we connect actively with young people on behalf of the Gospel mission, youth might feel greater acceptance, trust, and community-spirit. Yet, they might also begin to perceive that their God pays attention to them too and cares deeply for them (*Challenge* 6). This may not be simply consoling. It might in fact spur some of these young people, who feel both heard and valued, to reach out to others who, like them, are in perpetual need of human and divine care.

ADOLESCENTS HUNGER TO KNOW THAT LIFE HAS MEANING

A disturbing intuition that both adolescents and adults sometimes have is that life does not matter, that it has little or no purpose whatsoever. A recent novel with an apocryphal tone, *Operation Wandering Soul*, by Richard Powers, speaks powerfully and caringly about this (Powers 1993). The novel highlights how and why this intuition is growing stronger in our land. It metaphorically tells stories about children who simply, unbelievably disappear (like the children pictured on milk cartons) and of innocent youngsters who are prematurely toughened and aged by wandering far, among the powers that be, in our materialistic, income-driven culture. When a culture turns its weakest, most naive individuals into human prey, the novel says, there can be little sense of meaning beyond the sheer instinct to survive.

The document *The Challenge of Catholic Youth Evangelization* comments on this. It says some young people today fear:

> that their families, their relationships, their church, their future and even their lives do not matter. One challenge of youth ministry, therefore, is to provide a Gospel vision of life that identifies and calls into question the false messages contemporary society gives to what it means to be human. Meaning and purpose are found in the call to love, which is the fullness of our humanity, centered in God and expressed in love of others (*Challenge* 5).

The Gallup Institute acknowledges that research done on young Americans shows they often feel it is "very important" that life have meaning. However, it seems that pastoral ministries in Christian churches, in the U.S., are not doing so well overall with that key challenge mentioned above in the *Challenge* document. The Gallup organization recently noted that a high percentage of young persons now indicate "most churches and synagogues today are not effective in helping people find the meaning of life." In other words, a basic spiritual need is being met only partially, at best, by church ministries. In fact, Gallup's research continues to show that "significant numbers of teens find churches to be irrelevant, unfulfilling, and boring" (Gallup 12).

A recent study by the Search Institute, *The Troubled Journey*, focused on almost 47,000 young people, sixth through twelfth grade ages, in America. The goal of *The Troubled Journey* research was to gain a composite look at the basic attitudes and behaviors of youth in the U.S. Regarding experiences which either support youth or untrack youth in their search for life's purpose, the Search report noted:

> Only ten percent of students in this study meet what the study identified as minimal standards for overall well-being . . . We cannot be sure what long-term consequences are in store for the 90 percent who fail to meet the criteria. Fortunately, some will thrive. And some, unfortunately, will carry over into adulthood some scar or behavioral tendency that will stifle productivity. The personal loss for these adolescents may result in a future in which happiness, success, family life, and social relationships are less satisfactory than they could be (*The Troubled Journey* 9).

The staff at Search Institute recommends that leaders who serve in churches, schools, and family-serving agencies adopt a two-pronged approach to "alter the frequency with which adolescents make choices which compromise their health . . . jeopardize their future," or otherwise endanger their view of life as meaningful and purpose-filled. The first approach is one they call *prevention of deficits*. In other words, it is part of the calling of Christian ministers today to help adolescents—in any practical ways they can—avoid such life-depleting patterns as being alone at home, overexposure to television and hedonistic experiences, parental addiction and/or abusive behavior, negative peer influences, and self-absorbed attitudes. The complementary approach is one which Search Institute calls *promotion of assets*. Thus, it is part of Christian ministers' evangelizing mission to help adolescents—in all practical ways possible—to develop "positive relationships in (their) families, friendship groups, schools and the (wider) community" while, at the same time, also promoting within young people themselves those personal convictions, values, and attitudes which are life-enhancing, prosocial and fundamentally in harmony with the Gospel which Christians profess (*The Troubled Journey* 2–9).

Earlier we noted that kids tend to be concerned about having a happy family life today. *The Girl Scouts Survey on the Beliefs and Moral Values of America's Children*, published in 1990, commented on youth's spiritual search for meaning today by saying they "tend to be family-oriented and not work-oriented." In the *Girl Scout* studies, 35% of children surveyed chose getting married and having a good family life as their most important aspiration. Only 6% chose "having meaningful and challenging work" and only 7% chose "becoming an important person." Thirteen percent selected "being able to make a lot of money." Significantly, 21% said that a close relationship with God was their most important aim as they think about the future (*Girl Scouts* xviii). The survey commentary said:

> one thing is clear, the family has a decisive place in (youth's) world of meaning. The family—whatever its configuration—is the institution most children trust to solve America's problems. Marriage and a good family life is their chief priority as they face the future . . . (and) their greatest source of emotional support and moral guidance (*Girl Scouts* 102).

Apparently, anything we can do to both promote and support healthy relationships in adolescents' family households, today and tomorrow, and anything we can do to promote a close relationship between adolescents and their original parent will aide youth in their spiritual quest. Promotion and support of such relationships will help kids deflect life's absurdities and embrace human life's true meaning.

THEREFORE, ADOLESCENTS HUNGER FOR THE SACRED

Between childhood and adulthood profound changes often occur in the religious needs of human beings. As one recent report has noted,

> Between the simple clarity of childhood's view of life and the veiled mysteries of maturity comes adolescence—a complex, eventful, and relatively brief period . . . questions that once seemed easy develop complexity. Religious concepts simple enough for a child's understanding cannot sustain the weight of adult life experience (Search 51).

The Challenge of Catholic Youth Evangelization notes that adolescents, searching for fresh ways to be faith-filled, often experience a church out of touch with their real-life situations and a church community which doesn't even consistently practice what it preaches. However:

> young people continue to search for a faith that makes sense, provides direction and meaning, and that challenges. They are looking for a language to help them understand their experiences of God, searching for ways to deepen their experiences of the sacred, and seeking a community of people with whom to journey (*Challenge* 6).

Thus, adolescence is often a critical time of change and insight when it comes to Christian faith. About 70% of all Americans say they have experienced significant changes in their faith lives, on one occasion or another, often during adolescence. Frequently, young people need much help in comprehending the import of such experiences and in learning how to build on them (Gallup 14). Probably, the church's ministers—the ordained and the non-ordained alike—make common but faulty assumptions about the faith lives of adolescents and adults in their communities. For example, they might uncritically assume that adolescents don't need much personal assistance in understanding their spiritual questions and encounters. Or they might believe young Christians' prayer is more textured or sophisticated than it really is. Or they might uncritically assume that the baptized "out there" have more complete knowledge of their church's teachings and traditions than they actually do. In fact, some research indicates that mainstream Christians are often quite "uncertain about what (they) believe, let alone why (they) believe" (Gallup 14).

A lack of vigilance regarding youth's authentic, spiritual hunger for experiences of the mysterious and the holy has led church leaders to much recent hand-wringing over disturbing trends. The Gallup Institute remarks that inattention on the part of clergy and other church leaders, and general lethargy among Christian lay persons, has created something like "a huge spiritual vacuum" in our nation, one which has "a wide variety of bizarre spiritual movements . . . drawing in millions of unwitting and unsuspecting Americans," young and old alike (Gallup 14). Adolescents seem particularly vulnerable to such unusual movements, fundamentalist congregations, pentecostalist healers, itinerant charlatans and so on.

While many modern youth think the condition of the world is getting worse and many also believe life will be harder for them than it was for their parents, a surprising percentage of adolescents today, in some respects, remain "surprisingly religious," to borrow a Gallup phrase. Several key influences seem particularly helpful to them in their desire to experience the sacred and remain in touch with the Christian faith dimensions of their lives.

■ Parents, especially mothers, influence adolescents' hunger for the holy in a positive way when they faithfully model Christian values and behaviors, when parents consistently show adolescents—in word and deed—that religiousness in life matters, and when they consistently and honestly 'do as they preach' about Christian values (Search 53).

■ Church congregations, peers, and school communities influence adolescents' search for the sacred in positive ways whenever they provide a "warm, supportive atmosphere" which nurtures adolescents in faith (Search 53).

■ Adults influence adolescents' hunger for the sacred when they recognize that although kids' church attendance can stop at times kids' interest in the sacred, the spiritual, and the future remains alive. It can be of great help when adults walk with adolescents on the journey which causes them to "go away for awhile in order to get ready to come home" to their spiritual family (Search 53).

■ It also helps to have adult Christians prepared to welcome wayward, youthful journeyors back when the time is right.

ADOLESCENTS HUNGER FOR JUSTICE AND A CHANCE TO SERVE

As the new document *The Challenge of Catholic Youth Evangelization* puts it:

> The hunger for justice is perhaps the least obvious of the hungers of young people . . . (adolescents) are quick to point out the inequities of life in the distribution of goods, possessions and even opportunities. Directly and indirectly, they experience violence, hatred, and hurt. Our challenge is to not let this hunger for justice succumb to the societal pressures of materialism, consumerism, and individualism (*Challenge* 6).

According to some, there is room, not much—but a little room, for idealism and social commitment in the 1990s, on the part of youth. It seems today that teenagers in particular often appear "more interested in getting ahead in the world than in cleaning up its injustices" (Gelman 10). In the late '80s, among older high school students, global issues—such as hunger, poverty, and various pollutions—ranked close to last among teenagers' concerns. Nevertheless, some teenagers involve themselves often in good works nowadays. Causes addressed by youth today tend to be less glamorous than those of the late '60s and '70s. Recycling campaigns, tutoring programs, serving meals at homeless shelters, and various environment-awareness projects are forms of service adolescents favor. Is there a national groundswell among adolescents presently toward volunteerism and justice-oriented works? Some say there is no evidence of a groundswell (Gelman 16). Search Institute's data on *The Troubled Journey* of adolescents in mainstream America found that involvement in service (one hour or more per week), in causes related to justice and care for others, "is more common among girls than boys, and it decreases through high school—especially for boys . . ." (Search 1991).

On the other hand, the Gallup Institute's exhaustive studies of all types of American adolescents, through recent years, leads it to claim "the spirit of voluntarism and charity are alive and well. Even more (adolescents in the '90s) would volunteer their services if someone would just ask them to do so" (Gallup 10). In fact, some studies of adolescents' need for justice and right order in the world have concluded that the most successful youth programs are the ones that try to teach young people how to be young people who care.

> This goes beyond asking them to place their pennies and dimes in a collection plate. At an early age they may help clear the table at the church dinner. As teens, they may help rehabilitate a house for an elderly person or serve at a hospital. Later they may spend a season or a year at a church mission to help those in need (Gallup 18).

In commenting on the importance of addressing the human hungers to serve and bring about justice for others, a hunger present in many adolescents, the William T. Grant Commission on Work, Family and Citizenship maintained, "There is virtually no limit to what young people . . . can do, no social need they cannot help meet." Young people, the Grant Commission added,—who are given naturally to idealism and hope—should be challenged to "become contributors, problem-solvers, and partners with adults in improving their communities and the larger society" (Search 1991).

How must this be done within church-sponsored ministries? The *Challenge* document indicates that ministers who reach out to youth can help address the spiritual hunger in young people for right order and hope-filled service, first and foremost, by authentically proclaiming and living a Christian vision of justice for all. The *Challenge* states:

> The Gospel calls (all persons) to a vision where(in) all have access to the goods and resources of the world, where the poor and the marginalized become a priority, and . . . justice and peace are signs that the reign of God has broken through (*Challenge* 6).

The voice of contemporary social research adds wisdom to what the *Challenge* paper has to say. Social commentators speak about the powerful effects of "prosocial behaviors," such as service projects or one-to-one outreach to those in trouble, whether these behaviors are officially sponsored by church-related organizations or not.

> Prosocial behavior covers a wide range of human actions—helping people in distress, donating time or energy to voluntary service organizations, attempting to reverse . . . injustice or inequality . . . for the welfare of others. When it comes to raising healthy children, promoting prosocial behavior is important as preventing antisocial or health-compromising behavior. Acts of compassion help develop social competencies, positive values, and sense of purpose in life. Furthermore, prosocial behaviors may actually reduce risky choices. Students who engage in helping behavior on a weekly basis as shown . . . tend to be less likely that non-helpers to report risky behaviors (*The Troubled Journey* 7).

CONCLUDING NOTES: DEVELOPING A PREFERENTIAL OPTION FOR YOUNG PEOPLE

Which fundamental spiritual values do we hope will evolve in the life stories of those children and adolescents whom we presently know or to whom we will be soon introduced? A conserving Christian culture wants them to value self-restraint and a sense of appropriate boundaries. Other values as well. Self-esteem and compassion for others, for example. Love and commitment to others and to just causes. Christian hope, too, of course.

In each of these value areas, as recent research data and personal observations of youth , tell us, we have just cause to be concerned (Search 12).

A powerful, summary statement—one I also happened to stumble upon on the night of that "What are youth's spiritual needs?" conversation—says a genuine mouthful.

> To a certain extent . . . adolescents are mimicking values that are present in the society at large, embodied in social institutions (home, family, church), modeled by significant adults, and reinforced by the print and broadcast media. Everywhere there is a strong culture pressure toward individualism. A second factor has to do with neglect of our children. Simply put, children are not a national priority . . . Finally, youth are now exposed, largely via the mass media, to a variety of ideologies, worldviews, and styles of life, some of which are inimical to healthy development. Children no longer inherit a coherent value system from family and community (and) are cast adrift to make hit-or-miss choices among a variety of known value systems. In this kind of environment, it takes conscious effort by adults to enable youth to choose constructive, life-affirming values and reject the unbridled pursuit of individual aims (Search 13–14).

Ministries which best serve the spiritual and other hungers of adolescents today—and the hunger of families with adolescents too—tend to take certain crucial steps to give witness to a Good News story that liberates, consoles, and challenges young people to develop fundamental Christian values (Gallup 18–19). Such steps include:

- Above all, convincing young people that they can count on the love of God and the love of the members of their local faith community, no matter what happens;
- Accepting children and adolescents unconditionally, in a spirit of genuine friendship, care, and welcome, for who they are, what they now are, and for their gifts—not simply for what we want them to be; in concert with that, accepting young people and their family members, fully, no matter what their racial, economic, political, and religious backgrounds;
- Teaching youth the rudiments of Scripture and church traditions
- Providing adults to reach out to youth—adults who understand adolescents' needs, their problems, their hopes and who will clearly teach young people what is right and what may be wrong;

- Providing adults to children and adolescents (all ages) who mentor them well by remembering what it was like to be young but realize how different it probably is to be a young person today;
- Teaching young people Christian moral values and practices in order to help them take places in leadership, eventually, in the wider community;
- Giving young people meaningful opportunities to serve others in their local faith community and in other, broader social settings; and
- Sharing increased responsibilities for the Christian community with young people and authentically encouraging them to place their best energies into the causes and issues which the church addresses.

In 1979, the bishops of Latin America met in Puebla, Mexico. As both prophets and pastoral caregivers, they identified fundamental priorities for Christian ministry in the 1980s among the most uprooted members in contemporary Western society—the poor and the young. The Puebla documents struck a note similar to notes sounded in the recent publication of *The Challenge of Catholic Youth Evangelization*. The bishops said that there is no time like the present for "an overall pastoral approach"—essentially an evangelizing approach which starts with a renewed attempt to reach out to adolescents and stand with them in solidarity—which centers on sharing with youth "the truth about Jesus Christ, the truth about the church's mission, and the truth about the human being" (*Puebla* 269). They added the baptized must continue to have faith in young people, despite all the things which trouble us about the experiences and real hungers of adolescents in our time, because "they (youth) are a source of hope" for the church and because they "inject real dynamism into the social body, and especially the ecclesial body" (*Puebla* 270).

Since there are so many spiritual hungers in youth today, I think many find it hard to know just where to begin. As I write this, I wander back home to my neighborhood and to thoughts of Justin, Brad, Alicia, Gerald, Spencer, and oh so many others. It all begins far away from the pages of statistics and the freighted commentaries of those in the know about adolescents in pop culture. It all begins, and in some senses, ends up not far from home, in your own neighborhood and mine where real kids—kids with many needs and real spiritual hungers—can usually be found. If only we look about, and if only we take a step or two to approach them, introduce ourselves (in the name of the Lord), and spend a little time paying attention to them.

Two snippets about unplanned encounters with adolescents come to mind right now. One comes from Robert Coles, speaking about a female teenager doing pretty well. The first snippet starts with her words.

> I can take care of myself. I can handle some of this stuff (drug dealers near the school, the sexual pressures classmates have exerted on each other.) My mom is strong, and I've got her strength in me. And my dad is strong, and he watches out for me.

The young person speaking here is lucky in some ways but in jeopardy nonetheless, according to Robert Coles, based upon her description of her entire life. She needs deep emotional and moral support, and the "attentive, continuing concern of others—a community of caring individuals," true Christian neighbors, to "make up for what she lacked while growing up" (Coles 74). At one point, she has even wistfully wished that she could find "one strong, good person to lean on—and the person wouldn't disappear." Again, as we look at youth—not youth as some amorphous social grouping or set of empty stereotypes but as real, touchable human persons somewhere near your own doorstep or mine—we discover:

> Those (young people) who have been lucky not by dint of their parents' money or power, but (by adults') continuous affection and concern, their wish to uphold certain ethical principles and then to live them, rather than merely mouthing them—such youths are well able to handle some of the nonsense and craziness this later part of the 20th century has managed to offer us all (Coles 73).

The second snippet has as its setting a busy shopping mall. It is a brief story about a young male called Rocky.

> He was named Christopher in baptism but, lately, since he turned 15 or 16, he has been asking them all to call him Rocky C. He is full of questions today. Some whisper that he is full of dark secrets. He sits, in the mall, near the fountain by Sound Warehouse and Macy's. He sees some friends from school go cruising by. He feels lonely there, but only slightly. He needs to do the right thing. When he was pretty mad on Friday, Rocky C. had asked his teacher just why he should do what Jesus taught. His teacher shifted around a bit, then said some of Jesus' own followers had asked that too. One even cried "What about us? We've given it up to the max for you. We went with you, not the crowd. What's in this for us?" Rocky's teacher said Jesus calmed

them by saying they would find what they were searching for if they walked his way, really. No excuses, and no other promises, and no jive. And it wouldn't be so easy. Now, Rocky C. sits on a bench. Near the fountain. The music from the Warehouse is good. He is full of questions. Some whisper that he has deep, dark secrets to keep. He knows that he has important decisions to make. Soon. Time to get busy. But, for the moment, he just sits. And he listens.

Regarding the human quest, this story makes me think. Words of St. Augustine come to mind "Our hearts are restless, O God, until they rest in you!" And on another note this story makes me wonder. Who will be the next person, the next Christian evangelizing adult, to cross his star-crossed path and reach out to Rocky in a compassionate way? Maybe, ironically, it will turn out to be you. Then again, maybe it will be me. We can only hope and pray that there is no time like the present for such a Gospel-rooted encounter.

Works Cited

Bellah, Robert et al. *Habits of the Heart: Individualism and Commitment in American Life*. San Francisco: Harper & Row, 1985.

Coles, Robert. "The Long Obstacle Course Called Adolescence," *Youthworker* 6.1 (Summer 1989)

Elkind, David. *All Grown Up and No Place to Go*. Reading, MA: Addison-Wesley, 1984.

Gallup, George H. Jr. *The Religious Life of Young Americans*. Princeton, NJ: Gallup International Institute, 1992.

Gallup, George and Castelli, Jim. *The People's Religion: American Faith in the '90s*. New York: MacMillan, 1989. (See also George Gallup and Jim Castelli, *The American Catholic People*, New York: Doubleday, 1987.)

Gelman, David. "A Much Riskier Passage" *Newsweek* (Fall 1990, Special Issue).

Girl Scouts U.S.A. *Girl Scouts Survey on the Beliefs and Moral Values of America's Children*. New York: Girl Scouts U.S.A., 1990.

Healthy Communities; Healthy Youth: How Communities Contribute to Positive Youth Development. Minneapolis: RespecTeen/Search Institute, 1993.

Ianni, Francis A. J. *The Search for Structure: A Report on American Youth Today*. New York: Free Press, 1989.

National Federation for Catholic Youth Ministry. *The Challenge of Catholic Youth Evangelization.* Washington, DC: NFCYM Inc., 1993.

Powers, Richard. *Operation Wandering Soul.* New York: Morrow & Company, 1993.

Puebla and Beyond. Maryknoll, NY: Orbis, 1980.

Search Institute. *Source,* Volumes I-V 1985-1989. Minneapolis: Search Institute, 1990.

Search Institute. "Kids Who Care." *Source* VII Number 3 (December 1991).

The Troubled Journey: A Profile of American Youth. Minneapolis: RespecTeen/ Search Institute, 1990.

Wackerlin, Brad. "Against All Odds, I'm Just Fine" *Newsweek* (Fall 1990, Special Issue).

CHAPTER 5

PROCLAIMING THE GOOD NEWS TODAY

JOHN ROBERTO

Without explicit proclamation of the essentials of the Good News, there "is no true evangelization."

The message of the Christ Event is, indeed, good news: the news of God's powerful, saving love and Jesus as the ultimate revelation of that love. Jesus Christ is the Good News; he is the embodiment of God's all-embracing love.

—The Challenge of Catholic Youth Evangelization

THE NEED FOR A COMPELLING VISION OF THE CHRISTIAN LIFE

The challenge of evangelizing young people is clear: we are called to proclaim the Good News so that it responds to the lives and world of adolescents, invites their response, and empowers them to live as disciples *today*. However, there is an underlying assumption beneath this challenge that gets lost in the discussion of evangelizing activities and strategies. What exactly is it that we are called to proclaim? I know that we are supposed to proclaim the Good News, but what does that mean to the young people we work with today? It seems to me that if young people are going to become disciples we must present them with a compelling vision of the Christian life worthy of their commitment. It must be a vision which engages their hearts and minds. It must be a vision which captures their imagination and guides them in how to live as Christians in our world today.

Without a compelling vision to share with young people our evangelizing efforts will be in vain. And that, in fact, may be exactly what is happening today. It seems that an important part of youth's dissatisfaction with the Church stems from an absence of a *spiritually challenging* and *world-shaping vision* that meets their hunger for the chance to *participate in a worthy adventure*. Several years ago, a youth ministry think tank expressed the problem in this way,

> Our efforts have focused on devising strategies for keeping young people in the church because it is a place where they will be "safe" from the terrors of the street or the seductions of the shopping mall. Our hopes for them are modest and reasonable. For the most part, they mirror the expectations we have for ourselves. We ask no more than that they grow up to be "good" people—decent, law abiding, successful in their jobs and happy in their marriages. To this end, we program activities which are certainly wholesome, sometimes edifying, and almost always "fun." Conscientious youth ministers work hard to find ways to involve youth in worthwhile service projects, and often such projects—which yield concrete results to which we can point with pride—are very successful. Of course, some youth *do* remain in the church, and most of these do turn out to be "good" people. But many do not. They leave the church because it asks nothing significant of them. They leave the church because it is spiritually innocuous.

> Ultimately, the spiritual needs of youth transcend the legitimate requirements of wholesome companionship, entertaining events, and even worthwhile service projects. What they ask from the church is not so much something to *do* as something to *be*. Their lives are already awash with tasks and activities, all designed to help them succeed in life—a life filled with tasks and activities! Meanwhile, the fundamental need they have to commit themselves body and soul to some One who will ask everything from them and give everything in return goes unrecognized by adults

who themselves have been asked to give "much" but not all. The failure of the church to present its own unique task in the kind of sharply defined and utopian terms that are needed to capture the ardent imaginations of the young is often seen by them as an indication of its abdication to the comfortable standards of secular culture. As long as the churches continue to present the issues of discipleship in a context they find relatively manageable and unthreatening, youth will fail to find sufficient scope there for their very considerable zeal. We should not be surprised then, if they look elsewhere (Osmer 6–7).

Our evangelization efforts will succeed only if we have a *spiritually challenging* and *world-shaping vision* that engages young people and responds to their hunger for the chance to *participate in a worthy adventure*. In this essay I would like to suggest several elements of a compelling vision of the Christian life that has the potential for engaging young people and responding to their hungers. It is only an outline intended to spark your own thinking and to invite reflection upon your own efforts to proclaim the Good News to this generation of young people.

A GOSPEL VISION

The Challenge of Catholic Youth Evangelization outlines four key themes which guide an explicit proclamation of the Good News:

- **A God who loves us:** The doctrine of the Incarnation tells us that "the Word became flesh/and made his dwelling among us" (Jn 1:14). Jesus Christ is God and is, therefore, the most complete revelation of God. Jesus' life and ministry reveal a compassionate God. Young people need to hear of this God who cares and loves individually and specifically. Mistaken or false images of God must be replaced with one of a God who is actively present and involved in the lives of our young people.

- **Healing our humanity**: Jesus offers healing and forgiveness of sin to those whom he encounters. That offer needs to be communicated to our young people. Jesus can heal the gaps that are so prevalent in the lives of many young people. He can heal the breakdowns in their personal relationships, in their families, in themselves, and in their relationship with God. Jesus and his message can bring forgiveness and healing to young people's pains and wounds, revealing the power of God's love.

■ **The message and ministry of Jesus**: To embrace God's love as proclaimed and lived by Jesus is to accept the values that Jesus taught. "'I give you a new commandment: love one another. As I have loved you, so you also should love one another. This is how all will know that you are my disciples, if you have love for one another'" (Jn 13:34–35). The love to which Jesus calls young people is not a vague feeling but a very practical and visible concern and care for all and especially those who are neglected or oppressed by others. This compassion is integral to being a disciple of Jesus. We are challenged to enable young people to understand the meaning of discipleship and to invite them to respond as youthful and energetic disciples of Jesus Christ.

■ **A community of believers**: The journey of faith has both a personal and a communal dimension. Young people certainly need to search through their faith questions, but they are invited to do so with the support of the faith community. Young people are invited to join a community that strives to witness to authentic discipleship through its community life, personal prayer and community celebration, lifelong growth in faith, and lives of justice, service and peace. This is a community that celebrates its beliefs in and through its sacramental life, a celebration that culminates in the Eucharist (*Challenge* 15–16).

These four elements provide the framework. We still need to identify those specific values and principles which can be used in presenting young people with a compelling vision of the Christian life, one which responds to their lives today. As you read the following thirteen values or principles, all of which are at the heart of the gospel, consider the needs of young people today: for meaning and purpose in life, for a moral code to live by, for healthy and meaningful relationships, for an antidote to violence and a response to injustice, for an alternative to materialism and consumerism, and to make a difference in our world.[1]

1. **The call to love one another and ourselves**. Jesus said that our love for one another is sign by which others will know that we are his disciples (Jn 13:34–35). Jesus said that we need to love others as we love ourselves and to remember that we are always loved by God.

   Key Passages: Jn 13:34–35; Mt 22:34–40; Mk 12:28–34; Lk 10:25, Lk 10:25–37 (Good Samaritan)

2. **The call to love even our enemies**. "Love your enemies, do good to those who hate you, bless those who curse you, pray for those who abuse you . . . If you love those who love you," Jesus said,

"what credit is that to you? For even sinners love those who love them" (Lk 6:27, 32).

Key Passages: Lk 6:27–36; Mt 5:43–48

3. The call to forgive one another and always to seek reconciliation with one another. Jesus said that we cannot ask forgiveness for our own sins unless we are also ready to forgive those who sin against us (Mt 6:12). Jesus said that we should not presume to offer sacrifice to God unless and until we have been reconciled with our brother or sister (Mt 5:23–24).

Key Passages: Mt. 5:23–24, Mt 6:12–15; Lk 15:11–32 (Prodigal Son), Luke 11:4, Lk 17:4; Mt 18:21–22

4. The call to renounce revenge. "If anyone strikes you on the cheek," Jesus said, "offer the other also" (Lk 6:29).

Key Passages: Lk 6:27–36, Mt 5:38–48

5. The call to avoid judging and condemning others. "Do not judge," Jesus said, "and you will not be judged; do not condemn, and you will not be condemned. . . . First take the log our of your own eye, and then you will see clearly to take the speck out of your neighbor's eye" (Lk 6:37,42).

Key Passages: Lk 6:37–42, Mt 7:1–6, John 8:1–11 (Woman Caught in Adultery)

6. The call to avoid self-righteousness, presumption, and resentment toward others. Jesus repudiated the proud Pharisee (Lk 18:10–14) and the resentful elder brother in the parable of the prodigal son (Lk 15:25–30). He condemned those who try to shut the doors of the kingdom of God so that others could not enter it (Mt 23:13–15) and said the publicans and prostitutes would enter the kingdom before their detractors would (Mt 21:31–32).

Key Passages: Lk 15:25–30, Lk 18:10–15; Mt 6:2–4; Mt 21:31–32, Mt 23:1–33

7. The call to befriend those whom society looks down upon. Jesus made himself the friend of the outcasts (Mt 11:19) and did not avoid their company (Mk 2:16).

Key Passages: Mt 11:19; Mk 2:16–17; Lk 8:26–39 (Man with Demons) Lk 14:12–14; Lk 19:1–10 (Zaccheus); Jn 4:3–41 (Samaritan Woman)

8. The call to serve one another, humbly and unselfishly. Jesus gave us an example when he washed the feet of his disciples (Jn 13:4–17). "But when you give a banquet," he said, "invite the poor, the crippled, the lame and the blind. And you will be blessed because they cannot repay you, for you will be repaid at the resurrection of the righteous" (Lk 14:13–14).

Key Passages: Jn 13:4–17; Lk 14:12–14, Lk 22:27

9. The call to serve the poor. Jesus singled out the poor in the beatitudes, insisting that the reign of God will be theirs (Lk 6:20), as did Mary in her Magnificat: "He has brought down the powerful from their thrones, and lifted up the lowly; he has filled the hungry with good things, and sent the rich away empty" (1:52–53). Jesus' parable of Lazarus and the rich man (16:19–31) is particularly compelling. Indeed, Pope John Paul II frequently cites it in summoning the church to the service of the poor and powerless.

Key Passages: Lk 1:52–53, Lk 6:20, Lk 16:19–31 (Lazarus and the Rich Man); Mt 25:31–46

10. The corresponding call to beware of riches and the attachment to possessions. Jesus said it would be easier for a camel to pass through the eye of a needle than for a rich person to enter into the kingdom of God (Mk 10:25). He said that those who would be his disciples should be ready to sell all that they have and give to the poor (10:21).

Key Passages: Mt 6:24, Mt 19:16–30 (Rich Young Man); Lk 12:13–21 (Rich Fool), Lk 16:19–31 (Lazarus and the Rich Man), Lk 18:18–29 (Rich Ruler); Mk 10:17–31

11. The call always to be just in our dealings with others. Jesus attacked the scribes and Pharisees for straining at gnats and swallowing camels and for neglecting the weightier matters of the law, including justice first (Mt 23:23).

Key Passages: Mt 23:23–24; Lk 11:42; Mk 12:38–40

12. The call to pray always and with complete trust in God. Jesus said that we should pray in complete confidence to God, "Ask, and you will receive. Search, and you will find. Knock, and the door will be opened for you" (Mt 7:7).

Key Passages: Mt 6:5–15, 7:7–11; Lk 11:2–4, 11:9–13, 18:1–14.

The Sermon on the Mount (Matthew, chapters 4–6) and The Great Sermon (Luke 6:20–49) capture many of the values outlined above. They should have a privileged place in our evangelizing efforts. As William Loewe notes, "The (Great) Sermon makes four points with utter simplicity. Love everyone, especially those you would ordinarily consider enemies. Claim nothing as your own, but use all you are and all that you have to meet the needs of others. Forgive everyone everything. Judge no one but yourself" (Loewe 25).

A VISION FOR YOUNG PEOPLE TODAY

Reflecting on these Gospel imperatives and the hungers of young people, I would offer the following "vision" of the Christian life that could form the core of our evangelization efforts with young people. We need to challenge young people to:

- trust in God's unconditional love, acceptance, and forgiveness; to discover this loving God in prayer;
- find meaning and purpose for their life in a relationship with God through Jesus Christ;
- be peacemakers and promote reconciliation — to work for peace and healing in their relationships, community and world; to resolve conflicts nonviolently;
- be good stewards of God's creation—to share their personal talents and possessions, as well as the resources of the earth;
- live a life of simplicity freed from the pressures of materialism and consumerism;
- respect the human dignity, worth, and equality of *all* people—to recognize that all people are created in the image and likeness of God;
- work for social justice to ensure that the essential human and material needs of all people are met; to work toward a world freed of poverty and oppression of all kinds;
- be compassionate and serve those in need—to develop a special sensitivity to human suffering and fragility; to engage in actions to respond to those in need;
- develop loving relationships built upon care, compassion, commitment, faithfulness, honesty, and a concern for the other person;
- discover God in action today through their families and friends, through individuals and church communities who give witness to their faith in Jesus Christ.

If we proclaimed this vision clearly and passionately in everything we do, would our young people find answers to their hungers? Would they find sufficient scope for their energy and zeal? Would they feel they were participating in a worthy adventure that asked everything of them and gave everything in return? I think they would!

We must emphasize with our young people that following Jesus means absorbing his inclusive, compassionate, and just vision of life. We must remind them that Jesus called people to change their lives toward the vision of the reign of God—to change their ways to God's ways. We must demonstrate that accepting Jesus' vision of new life will bring them wholeness and liberation, and the certainty of being loved unconditionally and extravagantly by God. We must also support and encourage them when they realize that following Jesus is not without cost—that it will bring sacrifice. I believe that young people are ready for the challenge and are looking for churches to provide it.

BRINGING THE VISION HOME

This brings us to the most important questions in this essay: What is *your* vision of the Christian life? What is the vision you are sharing with young people through your ministry? What are you proclaiming in your evangelization efforts? It's time to check. We need to examine critically how our evangelization efforts (programs, activities, relationships) and our entire ministry communicate a vision of the Christian life in keeping with the Gospel imperatives. Consider the following steps:

- Think about your own personal vision of the Christian life and how you are concretely living this vision today. Spend some time reflecting on the Gospel passages included with the Gospel imperatives in this essay.
- Reflect on the vision already embedded in your evangelization efforts and in your ministry-wide programming. Identify the dominant characteristics or elements of the Christian vision already in your ministry.
- Gather your leadership team (adults and youth) and invite them to reflect on their personal vision of the Christian life and on the ministry-wide vision. Use the activity above to help you with the ministry-wide vision.
- Review the hungers of youth in *The Challenge of Catholic Youth*

Evangelization and in chapter four of this book. Invite the team to identify the most important hungers of youth in your community.

■ Invite your team to reflect on the Gospel imperatives in this essay. Organize your leaders into reflection groups to read and reflect on the Gospel passages.

■ Develop a statement of your ministry's vision of the Christian life and how it responds to the hungers of youth, using the team's reflections on their personal visions, the ministry-wide vision, and the Gospel passages.

■ Use this vision of the Christian life as the core content for all your evangelization and ministry efforts as you plan, conduct, and evaluate programs and activities. Use this vision as a primary tool in all your adult and youth leadership training.

CONCLUSION

Several years ago, during the III Encuentro process, young people articulated a compelling vision of the Christian life which summarizes very well what I have tried to express in this essay.

> First of all, we announce the option for peace as against violence (Mt 26:51; 2 Cor 5:18); for love as against injustice (Jn 15:17); for good as against evil (Dt 30:15); for the family as a fundamental value through which faith is transmitted (Eph 6:4); and for maintaining one's own culture.

> Likewise, we denounce materialism, which leads us to believe that the important thing in life is to have more and more in contrast to the teachings of the Gospel (Mt 6:25–30; *Populorum Progressio*, no. 19).

> We denounce the hunger and poverty that our people, with whom Jesus identifies, suffer (Mt 25:31), the violence (Mt 26:52), and the arms race (*The Challenge of Peace*, no. 204); we are opposed to any use of nuclear weapons (no. 215).

> We denounce abortion, the abuse of drugs and alcohol, and the negative and manipulative influence of commercial propaganda that creates false needs.

We do not just denounce these injustices, we also feel ourselves called to struggle for peace in the world, to live a more simple life style in solidarity with our poor brothers and sisters, and to reach out beyond our nationalities, races, languages, and socio-economic levels so as to be really one Catholic family.

Let us be aware that we can change the world with our way of life today. (*Prophetic Voices—The Document on the Process of the III Encuentro Nacional Hispano de Pastoral* 12)

End Notes

[1] These key values are taken and/or adapted from Richard McBrien's article, "Issues Consuming Church not Gospel Imperatives" in *National Catholic Reporter*, August 26, 1994.

Works Cited

The Challenge of Catholic Youth Evangelization. National Federation for Catholic Youth Ministry. New Rochelle, NY: Don Bosco Multimedia, 1993.

Loewe, William. "The New Christologies." CHURCH, Volume 3, Number 4, Winter 1987.

Prophetic Voices -- The Document on the Process of the III Encuentro Nacional Hispano de Pastoral. Washington, DC: USCC Publishing, 1986.

INTRODUCTION TO
PART TWO

THE PRACTICE OF CATHOLIC YOUTH EVANGELIZATION

PART TWO OF THIS *GUIDE* begins with an essay by **Jeffrey Johnson** on the dynamics of Catholic youth evangelization. Building his essay on his own life story, the author examines practical issues such as the nature of adolescent evangelization, the relationship of evangelization and catechesis, and the theological groundwork of all evangelization, the Incarnation of the Word. He goes on to explore the essential principles and dynamics of youth evangelization, noting the importance of relationships in evangelization ministries, importance of team approach to evangelization, and the critical need to personally invite young people into "moments of recognition" and conversion to the gospel message. This chapter concludes with reflections on the element of the entire evangelizing process known as proclamation and details specific ideas on how to design evangelizing proclamation experiences for groups of young people.

The next chapter, Chapter Eight in this book, presents another contribution by **Reynolds R. Ekstrom**. This essay examines passages from the document, *The Challenge of Catholic Youth Evangelization*, which pertain to the compelling characteristics of the evangelizing community and elaborates on a number of these unique characteristics. The piece then takes a close look at the many collaborative partnerships which should be formed, at the level of the local faith community, in order to faithfully and effectively fulfill the mission of Catholic youth evangelization today. The chapter culminates with a number of pointed, challenging questions on which local ministry team members would do well to contemplate.

The final chapters in Part Two are focused on how to empower adults and young people for the mission of Catholic evangelization today. The piece on empowering adults is written by **Reynolds R. Ekstrom**. It investigates various means by which adult members of parish, school, and other local Christian bodies can be and should be prepared for sharing the Word with adolescents today through outreach and proclamation of the gospel. The essay on empowering young people to become bearers of the Word is contributed by **Rev. Gilberto Cavazos**. He shares his parish experience in preparing young people for evangelizing ministry. Fr. Cavazos, in doing so, also reflects on why youths should be called to evangelize their peers and how the youth evangelization efforts, known as *La Tropa de Cristo* in his parish, lends readers many examples on how young people can be moments of grace for others.

CHAPTER 6

THE DYNAMICS OF CATHOLIC YOUTH EVANGELIZATION

JEFFREY JOHNSON

Efforts in Catholic evangelization of young people include the elements of witness, outreach, proclamation, invitation, conversion and the call to discipleship. Theoretically, these elements can be seen as taking place sequentially. However, evangelization is rarely a linear process.

Accepting and responding to the call to discipleship is the culmination of the process of evangelization. However, the dynamics of evangelization are interrelated, and the process itself is cyclic in nature. Witnessing to the Good News is always an important aspect of daily Christian living. Intentional outreach to unchurched or unGospeled young people is an ongoing challenge. The proclamation of the Good News is continual, and the invitation into relationship is constantly renewed. Conversion, too, is a cyclic process that takes place again and again as turning points and "aha moments" recur in the lifelong process of growth in relationship with Jesus and the community of believers. All these elements together result in a lifestyle of discipleship.

—The Challenge of Catholic Youth Evangelization

MY STORY: A CCD DROP-OUT MAKES GOOD

I was evangelized by the Protestants, with the help of my older sister. When I was entering high school, my sister told me "Go to Young Life, it's cool." These were NOT words of invitation . . . "Please come with me" . . . since being seen with a younger brother would damage her social standing with her friends. These were words of advice, casual crumbs dropped in the hope that this group could transform me from total nerd to social acceptability. And so I went.

My first impression of that crowded living room was "Wow! Wall-to-wall Teenagers!" I soon got into the music being pounded out on the piano (Yes, there was youth ministry *before* guitars) and recognized a few friends from junior high. There was a skit that made us all laugh, some more singing and then one of the leaders stood up to give what I learned was a regular feature—a ten minute talk on basic Christianity. Andy and Jack were not the stereotype youth ministers of today—they were my family dentist and a public high school principal. This took a little getting used to, but I soon became a regular at Young Life.[1]

My last bout with religious instruction was 6th grade CCD classes which met on Saturday mornings, not the highlight of my week. I quit immediately after Confirmation that year and breathed a sight of relief that I was religiously educated for life. However, those Young Life talks revealed a much different God than I hear about at mass on Sunday. I became intrigued with the stories of Jesus, his humanity and God's desire for a relationship with me. On a winter retreat I heard a young man named John stand up and give a testimony about the difference God had made in his life. That was it! That's what I wanted and soon I joined the Bible study group, learned to pray in my own words, enjoyed the fellowship but struggled to integrate it all with the pre-Vatican II parish mass.

My Irish Catholic mother, perhaps fearful that I would stray from the One, True Church, sent me back to CCD my junior year. The year was 1964 and the decor was predated only by the teacher's methodology. Out of the depths of my boredom came the thought: The Holy Roman Catholic Church must renew itself and learn how to evangelize its baptized, uncommitted members! . . . or something like that. Actually, I just wondered why the Church could not do something like Young Life and soon I got the chance to try. The first years of youth ministry challenged me to translate my Young Life experience in high school and college into a Catholic parish setting. This article is an attempt to articulate the principles of evangelization as they apply to contemporary Catholic youth ministry.

WHAT IS EVANGELIZATION?

Evangelization is not a methodology for membership drives in the Catholic Church or gimmicks for getting kids to come to our youth programs. *Evangelii Nuntiandi* states: "For the Church, evangelizing means bringing the Good News into all the strata of humanity, and through its influence transforming humanity from within and making it new" (#18). To bring Good News to the strata of humanity we call adolescents, we must *be* Good News. To a young person whose life is filled with adults in authority positions, good news is someone who will listen and offer a trust relationship. From that caring relationship we proclaim verbally and non-verbally the astounding truth that God loves teenagers. The settings are as varied as our ministries, but contain the common element of an adult willing to relate without an agenda, to care without conditions, to love like God, with no strings attached.

The Relationship of Evangelization and Catechesis

In *A Vision of Youth Ministry*, one of the seven components of youth ministry is the ministry of the Word. "The ministry of the word is the sharing with others of the Gospel message, the good news of God's love and salvation as shown to us in Jesus Christ. This sharing involves elements of what are commonly known as evangelization and catechesis" (7). It is essential to see these as two part of a whole process of faith growth. I believe that our personal experiences of being evangelized and catechized deeply influence our perceptions of these different ministries. Our own conversion experiences implant the instincts with which we approach ministry. We must also remember that differences in style do not lessen the validity of other approaches. A multiplicity of approaches are needed to reach the variety of needs among today's youth.

In Robert Hater's, *The Relationship Between Evangelization and Catechesis,* he observes two general approaches:

The first sees evangelization (including pre-evangelization) as operative before a person makes a commitment of faith, and catechesis as taking over after a person has made an initial act of faith. This approach can easily dichotomize evangelization and catechesis. The second sees catechesis as one element—a very important one—in the evangelization process. Seen in this way, evangelization and catechesis both are intimately related, but evangelization is more fundamental" (1–2).

The first approach can be seen in the *Sharing the Light of Faith (National Catechetical Directory)*, which states that "Catechesis presupposes prior pre-evangelization and evangelization" (#34). In the more recent document, *The Challenge of Adolescent Catechesis*, evangelization is described as foundational to catechesis. "Through evangelization we invite young people into the community of faith, into a faith relationship with Jesus Christ, and into the lifestyle of the Good News. Catechesis, then builds upon this faith by explaining more fully the Good News and by exploring the common faith that binds the Catholic Christian community together" (6). This approach is the most widely held within youth ministry since it fits the experience of youth and youth-serving ministers. Within this approach, "Evangelization invites persons to the community of faith; catechesis explores the common faith that binds the community together" (Warren 75). Evangelization proclaims the Good News, catechesis explains the Good News (Zanzig 33). This distinction is most obvious in the following graphic of Don Kimball's wedge model in which he identifies the conversion experiences or "Aha" moments as the catalysts for catechesis (111–147).

Evangelization describes those activities that reach out to untouched youth and initiate relationships of trust. These one-to-one relationships become the building block of community within which the Gospel is proclaimed, verbally and non-verbally. Within individual relationships or group settings, the young people have conversion experiences that awaken a hunger to grow in their new found faith.

Kimball's wedge model reflects the ministry process and accompanying programs of the Rite of Christian Initiation of Adults (RCIA). A significant difference between the two is that the RCIA presupposes a community and in youth ministry a community must usually be built. The wedge model may be particularly helpful to those parishes designing Confirmation programs based on the RCIA process, for it clarifies the nature of the community building necessary before conversion and meaningful catechesis.

The second approach to the relationship of evangelization and catechesis is worth noting because it appears in *Evangelii Nuntiandi* and *Catechesi Tradendae*. In brief, this view holds that "Evangelization is the energizing center of the Church's pastoral ministry" (Hater 17–18). Catechesis, then, "specifies evangelization. It is the moment or element in the evangelization process which invites a person to hear, understand, interiorize, and respond to God's Word in acts of service and celebration" (Hater 18). In this view, evangelization is the activity whereby the spiritual energy released from proclaiming the Gospel revitalizes all the ministries of the Church. Both perspectives are essential. For our purposes in this chapter, we will focus on the first approach.

THE INCARNATION: A THEOLOGICAL BASIS FOR EVANGELIZATION

The theological basis and inspiration for evangelization comes from the doctrine of the incarnation. In the Prologue of John's Gospel, we read: "The Word became a human being and full of grace and truth lived among us" (John 1:14). The Son of God became human in the flesh of Jesus. The phrase "he lived among us" can be translated "he pitched his tent among us." The Son of God is not here to visit, but to stay, to live among us, with us, as we live. In the life and ministry of Jesus we recognize God's promise of presence, Emmanuel, God-with-us, in a form we can understand.

This kind of theology talks geography. The incarnation reveals that God is willing to come to our turf, to experience all of life with us. Jesus bids us to love other as he has loved us. Within youth ministry, we adopt Jesus' style with the "incarnational approach" of going to the young people, to their turf, to communicate in ways they will understand.

This incarnational approach is apparent in the story of Jesus' encounter with the two disciples on the road to Emmaus (Luke 24:13–35). It is appropriate that this story was chosen to illustrate the dynamics of youth ministry in the *A Vision of Youth Ministry*. The two disciples resemble today's young people—on the move and so absorbed in their own problems and confusion that they did not recognize Jesus Christ, who they knew. Jesus joins them on the road, falling in step with them, observes their intensity and takes the risk to ask what was received as a stupid question. However, as the two sense the stranger's sincerity, they stumble over each other to tell their story of crushed hopes about the Messiah. Jesus carefully listens to their stores before responding with Scripture and tradition, opening their eyes to the deeper meanings of the experiences. It is only during the celebration that the two disciples realize who Jesus is and immediately find him gone from their sight. Their instant reaction is to return to their friends and tell them of their discovery, recalling how their hearts were burning as they talked with Jesus on the road.

Adopting this incarnational style with young people means that we, too, join them on their journey, not expecting them to come to us. We take the risk to ask questions in an attempt to show interest in their lives. When we have won their trust, we offer the richness of Scripture and Catholic tradition in manageable pieces that will shed light on their questions and struggles. A few will recognize God's presence within the relationship that gets built, other will recognize God's loving activity long after they have left us, and still others may never know the source of our concern for them.

Jesus and Paul both used the rabbinic tradition of teaching with their lives. How they lived meant as much as what they said. Paul describes this lifestyle of incarnational ministry in 1Thessalonians 2:8: "Because of our love for you we were ready to share with you not only the Good News from God but even our own lives. You were so dear to us!" In youth ministry we give others not only our words, but our lives in relationships. Young people want to be real and demand the same authenticity of us, which requires extra sensitivity to the congruency of our teachings and lives. The incarnational approach invites us to make our lives the vehicle for ministry, the main tool for communicating God's love for young people.

In 1Corinthians 9:20–23, Paul writes: " . . . While working with the Jews, I live like a Jew in order to win them . . . when working with Gentiles, I live like a Gentile . . . Among the weak in faith, I become weak like one of them . . . " To identify with young people does not mean to become a teenager, imitating their slang and dress styles. Rather it means to become fluent in their language and culture. Recognizing that youth live in a quasi-subculture is not to revive the generation gap or polarize youth form adults, but to acknowledge the need to communicate in ways that they will understand. As Paul used the image of the "Unknown God" to communicate with the sophisticated Greeks in Athens, we search youth culture for images and symbols that reveal God's love for them (Acts 17:16–34).

One of the most imaginative examples of this incarnational style I have heard was the following story of a high school counselor named Mary. She seemed unable to reach a certain group of girls at her high school and in deep frustration finally asked one of these girls what the problem was. The girl blurted out, "Well, just look where you are!" Mary was sitting behind her desk, in the air-conditioned office, across the hall from the Dean of Women where these girls regularly visited for disciplinary reasons. So Mary did some research and discovered that this group hung out around the cafeteria door that led to the parking lot. it was hot and unpleasant, but being near the boiler room, they could smoke and skip classes easily.

Over the summer Mary moved her office . . . to the boiler room! She had to work through all sorts of red tape with her principal and school board members who assured her it was very unprofessional, but she did it. Relationships started clicking as kids realized that she was serious about being their friend. Her nickname soon became "Moms," even though she was the same concerned person as before. All that had changed was geography. It convinced those girls that she would do what was necessary to have a relationship with them.

One can imagine a modern day Kenosis-like hymn sung in her praise: "She was a professional but did not cling to air-conditioning . . . " (apologies to Philippians 2:5–11)

An essential part of the Good News we have to share is that the incarnation is not a one time event. As James Nelson writes, . . . "the Word, God's dynamic, life-shaping presence, not only *became* flesh two millennia ago but also *becomes* flesh now" (18). This means that our flesh and our lives are the medium for God's love. It means that the lives of the young people with whom we minister carry God in *their* flesh. But just as the disciples on the road to Emmaus were blinded by the immediacy of their own needs, we all need others to coax us into recognizing our goodness, our Godness. If we take the incarnation seriously, we must believe in our goodness and the goodness of the young. If God lives within young people, active in their relationships, then our ministerial task is not to bring God to youth, but to join God in loving them. As Don Kimball has written in his book *Power and Presence: A Theology of Relationships,*

> In the Incarnational perspective, God is already present from the beginning of a person's life, and salvation is an ongoing series of deepening discoveries of his presence, and an ongoing series of yeses, leading to a more profound friendship with God. As this relationship develops, the power of the Lord works through the individual and the mighty works of the Lord be-

come apparent. You "will do even greater works that I have"
(John 14:12). (54)

True evangelization involves a personal encounter with God in which
Gospel values become the primary influence on one's decisions and relationships. The Good News is that God loves me and the surprising news is
that God wants to love others through me! This means that saying yes to
God will not solve all our problems or meet all our needs, but will demand
a conscious responsibility to care more for others than ourselves. One of
the delightful surprises of Christianity is that in serving others in a healthy
way we can lessen our own neediness. As Jesus put it, "For whoever wants
to save one's life will lose it, but whoever loses one's life for my sake will
save it" (Luke 9:24).

Becoming a committed Catholic Christian means embracing all the
Gospel values, including peace-making and justice. In 1971, the world
Synod of Bishops clearly stated that justice is a constitutive element of the
proclamation of the Gospel. This means that working for peace and justice
is integral to discipleship. One cannot be a follower of Jesus Christ if he or
she does not seek to live and work for justice and peace. Bringing this
challenge to young people means that our relationships must model the
compassion, acceptance and equality that Jesus taught and lived. As adult
leaders, we must imitate Jesus' generosity, especially in his ability to love
the unlovable. Faith in Jesus Christ means more than selecting some com-
forting words or ideas that support my chosen lifestyle and that meet my
personal needs. Faith involves the embrace of Jesus' total message, especially the parts that challenge our attitudes and lifestyles.

PRINCIPLES OF EVANGELIZATION

A ministry of evangelization involves methods of outreach, initiating
and building relationships, working with a concern for conversion experiences. The following section contains practical strategies and reflective
questions designed to enable youth ministers to apply these principles to
their local youth ministry settings.

Principle 1—Outreach: From Neutral Turf to Holy Ground

The incarnational approach provides motivation to *go to* young people where they are living their lives. A few generations ago the locus of social interactions was the church. This is still often true in some small towns and urban neighborhoods today. The relationships of youth as well as adults intersected at church. Today's communities look much different. The focal point for young people's lives is not the Church, yet many adults believe that youth ought to go to church and church events as they once did when they were young. To expect this is to work against the sociology which says that the focus of young people's lives is the high school or extensions of the high school subculture. Therefore, the first steps of outreach ministry is being an "amateur sociologist" and identifying the focal points for youth in your community.

Where do young people spend their time?

The local fast food joints, the shopping center, the streets, certain parks are all examples of geographic locations within a community. The same is true within the high school building. If you have access to the school during school time, you can hang out at the right time and place to meet kids. Observe the sociology of a high school lunchroom—the different groups, the loners, the rules and roles that regulate the interaction. The same principle applies to any ministry setting, whether rural, city or suburban. Identify where the kids are and be there.

What are the groupings of youth within your parish, youth ministry or high school(s)?

Identify the leaders and followers, whether each is open or closed, what rules and roles operate in each group, their interrelationships and influence within the group, etc. To be ignorant of these dynamics is to limit one's ability to communicate and minister with each group.

What are the boundaries of your ministry?

Do you focus on one group, only kids from your own parish, or denomination, or a particular high school, favor girls over guys or vice versa, leadership versus follower type kids, etc. Evangelization implies that we are first aware of our own self-imposed limitations and reach out beyond the boundaries present in our ministry. Later we will discuss the role of the youth ministry team in helping each other recognize their limits and challenging each other to grow beyond them.

To accomplish this informal sociological research, look to those already knowledgeable about the youth of your community. When I began to focus on a brand new high school, I asked the principal to identify the three teachers in the school with the closest relationships with students. I spent an hour with each of them, asking their observations on the "community" I was entering, focusing especially on unmet needs. I learned more in those three hours than I would have in three months of stumbling around the high school. Others to interview include other youth workers, counselors, pastors, police, social workers, parents, and of course, the youth themselves.

One of the benefits of outreach ministry is how it changes young people's concept of church. I was once helping a couple prepare music for their wedding and listened as the young man introduced me to his fiancee. "This is Jeff, he sings at church on Sunday and hangs around the high school for the kids who need him." The implication was that he never "needed me" but knew I was available for others. It meant something to him that his church was providing someone to be there. Our presence in the high school world can be an extended arm of the Church, reaching out in concern for ones who otherwise may never be touched. As difficult it is to measure, outreach ministry offers our presence and availability in the high school scene, time-consuming yet valuable gifts to adolescents.

Where does your ministry happen?

This is the crucial question. Young people often perceive church as an adults-only experience and church property and programs as adult territory. It is essential to meet young people away from our office of programs where we are *not* in charge. When we are on neutral turf, relationships can happen more easily, without roles, especially authority roles. Young people are attracted to real human beings, not adults playing roles. This incarnational step makes us more vulnerable by being on neutral territory or on their turf, where they are most comfortable. This non-verbally says, "I am here to relate."

An example of outreach ministry that worked for me was the Friday morning Breakfast Club. There was a group of seniors at the high school who were not interested in a Bible study or anything religious, but were getting bored with the regular youth group. My wife Carmen and I were concerned about losing the relationships, so we created a vehicle to stay in touch during their last year of school. We met for breakfast every Friday morning at a restaurant. The only "religious" thing we did was say grace. The numbers varied from week to week with as many as twelve youth participating. The Breakfast Club was successful because it was an adult activity they enjoyed, and there was no pressure to do or be anything. At the end of the year they went off to college and we slept in on Fridays.

One of the girls led a wide lifestyle during her first two years of college. During her junior year she began to get involved with the Church again. She called to get together with us and tell us about her experiences. We invited her over to the house, but she suggested that we go out to lunch instead. Where? The restaurant, the holy place, where she had experienced faith with us.

Henri Nouwen tells of a more intense and intimate friendship in which his friend tells him, "From now on, wherever you go, all the group between us will be holy ground" (31). We pitch our tents on that neutral turf, believing that some of it will be transformed by God into holy ground.

Principle 2—Relational Ministry: "Friend-Makers for God"

The phrase relational ministry is redundant because by nature all ministry is relational. Ministers with youth must believe that faith is best communicated through personal relationships. If our relationships are the primary vehicle for communicating faith, then initiating new relationships is essential to successful evangelization. Once we place ourselves in the world of the young, how do we go about building relationships?

First, we need to realize that small talk is a necessary tool of evangelization of youth. I learned this because of a guy I will call Bill. During my first year of youth ministry his girlfriend became pregnant and Bill's parents reacted by grounding him for the entire summer. I was not close to Bill but visited him on a regular basis that summer. I was inexperienced and uncertain of how to discuss the pregnancy, so we never actually talked about it. Instead we talked about everything else. The following fall I was talking to one of Bill's friends at school. He said that Bill told him about how I had talked Bill out of running away from home last summer. I smiled, knowing that we had never talked about that, but somewhere in our small talk he made the decision not to run away from home.

It is ironic that we worry about what to say when our interest and concern is communicated so well non-verbally. All of us have favorite teachers from high school who we can describe perfectly, but could not remember one of their profound words. It is the presence of a person, their care for us, that makes the greatest impact. We truly underestimate the power of our small task.

The second practical strategy is to get involved in the interests of youth or get them interested in your activities. This means to show an interest in the events of the high school, their work, families, sports, whatever involves them. Most of us enjoy talking about ourselves and our hobbies, accomplishments and hopes. In the simple asking of questions can we show concern about their life and learn where they are invested—sports, drama, cars, clothes, music.

The reverse also works. I enjoy music—making it, listening to it, browsing record stores, and find it easy to relate to youth in this area. This includes providing guitar lessons, attending concerts, listening to records or just talking about our favorite rock groups. My wife has developed a group of girls by teaching them to quilt or do other crafts and gradually deepened the involvement into discussion groups and Bible studies. I know of youth workers who have volunteered to teach, coach, chaperone at high school classes and events, especially when they cannot visit the school during hours. The principle is simple—identify the gifts that the youth have (or we have) and design activities around those interests. Then allow the relationships to happen.

One example of this principle was a group from the music room at the high school. The music room was a small auditorium with low lights and rock music that was off-limits to teachers. It was the perfect place to escape the pressures of high school life. I regularly spent time there and got to know a group of youth who were definitely not "church" youth. A few of them had come to one youth meeting and that was enough for them. So I developed the relationships around rock music by inviting them to help me with a radio program at the local station. For thirty minutes we would play a record, say "heavy and relevant" things, play another record and say "heavy and relevant" things. The only "rule" was that they clean up their language, since it was a live show. After the show we would go out for pizza. One night we had a beautiful conversation about sex, dating, marriage and love. These young people would never have come to a youth night on "Christian Sexuality" at church, but it sure happened at Sammy's pizza.

There are many young people who rarely or never participate in church worship services or youth programs, but the relationships we build with them are as holy and meaningful as the ones with leadership youth. We must continue to be strong advocates for outreach ministry so that the rest of the Church learns to value all youth, whether they make a contribution to our church or not. Jesus placed a high priority on ministry with people at the fringe of Jewish society, yet he never neglected his core group. We can do the same.

Paul writes in 2 Corinthians 5:17–21 that we are to be "ambassadors for Christ." The *Good News Bible's* version translates that as "friend-makers for God," a marvelous image for outreach, relational ministers. The crucial reflective questions for relational ministry are:

- How do you make friends?
- How did your closest friend become close?
- What kind of young people are you naturally attracted to?
- What kind are naturally attracted to you?
- Who do you have trouble relating with?

Another fun exercise is to remember what kind of high school kid you were. Who were your friends? What were your interests? How would you fit into the group that you are presently involved with? Would you come to your own program? The bottom line is: Do young people become friends because of your program or in spite of it? The Gospels and New Testament Church gives us numerous examples of "programs" being created out of the existing relationships, based on the gifts and needs present. By reflecting on our past and present relationships we can learn how we best relate with youth, what approaches and programs foster those relationships and how a team can best be structured to meet the most needs.

Principle 3–Team Ministry: ". . . the Body should work together as a whole, with all the members in sympathetic relationship with one another." (1 Corinthians 12:25)

Since the ministry of evangelization must be committed to outreach and deeply rooted in relationships, it naturally follows that team ministry is essential for successful evangelization. As the high school youth culture fragments into smaller sub-groups, we need more ministers to reach out to those groups. We minister best according to our natural gifts and personalities. Therefore, we need a team within which we can discern how best to serve. This variety of gifts and needs dictates a multiplicity of approaches to evangelize both untouched and alienated youth. The task of team is to unify the diversity of ministries.

Paul provides us with a veritable textbook on team ministry in 1Corinthians 12, declaring each community to be called into the same internal unity as the human body. This 2000 year old letter addresses the freshest of issues—that all gifts come from the same Spirit, that the most beautiful parts are as necessary as the less attractive ones, that parts of the body cannot discount each other's importance and that no one has all or even most of the gifts. In other words, we need each other to do what God wills for our ministry. Ultimately, all gifts serve the highest gift, which is love.

A variety of ministers are needed to reach out to the various groups within a high school—the preppies, the jocks, the burn-outs. The sociology of youth culture requires that we offer a variety of approaches to reach these different groups and individuals. To reach out as a team also makes a statement about the nature of Christianity, that believers pray, work, and sometimes live in community.

Equally important is the fact that evangelization needs the other ministries to fulfill its mission. Without catechesis, carefully nurtured conversion experiences can lose their life-changing power. Without worship, community-building, justice and service, and healing the seeds of faith soon wither and fade into dormancy.

The Church of Our Saviour in Washington D.C. is built on this concept of gifts. Each member of this church belongs to a mission group which has a special ministry focus—the aged, youth children, education, and social work in the poor sections of the city. The community spends much time and energy discerning their members gifts, based on their vision of church. In *The Eighth Day of Creation*, originally written as a guide for the various mission groups, Elizabeth O'Connor offers a deeply spiritual, yet practical, guide to discovering one's creativity and gifts for ministry. (55) In the reflective exercises in this book, she asks the reader to consider their gifts, the risks and sacrifices of developing their gifts, and what obstacles stand in the way of their full use. These are the questions we need to ask ourselves in the Church, not just within our youth ministry teams. Such a New Testament model of church can inspire all parish communities to call forth its gifts. The interest in peer ministry among youth is evidence that all members benefit from mutual examination of gifts.

The critical reflective questions for team ministry include:

■ With whom do you minister?
■ Are you part of a team with a variety of gifts and approaches or are you going it alone?
■ Have you identified your own gifts?
■ How much do you expect of each other?
■ Do you spend sufficient time together outside planning and conducting programs to call yourself a team?
■ Do you celebrate your ministry together?

Principle 4—Conversion: "All Ministry is Invitation"

Evangelization is always focused toward providing conversion experiences. In *Evangelization and Catechesis*, Johannes Hofinger describes conversion as a "turning-around to a better way of life" . . . "toward God as the goal and meaning of his entire human life" (33–34). The true mark of a conversion is change. "The profound change which is characteristic of any genuine conversion can be considered in two ways. On the one hand, it means a break with the past; on the other, it means a further growth of the good already present in the convert before his conversion, although it might not have been in the foreground" (34). Whether this change is dramatic and public or quiet and private, any genuine encounter with God produces change in a person's life.

The word conversion carries multiple meanings. For this reason Tom Zanzig chooses the phrase "moment of recognition" for this experience. This phrase is helpful in that it includes the prior experience of a young person as contributive toward the immediate change. He writes, "All that has been known by us before—our experiences of the symbols and rituals of our faith, the witness of Christian parents, prior religious education, and so on—are at some point in time understood as integrated and personally meaningful realities (33).

Many Catholics are uncomfortable with the notion of conversion when associated with evangelicals, especially fundamentalists. Some Christians experience a dramatic, one-time decision for Christ and structure their ministry around the necessity for others to make a public declaration of Jesus Christ as their personal Lord and savior. The predominant Catholic (and mainline Protestant) perspective emphasizes a more gradual conversion process that involves a progression of faith within which there are *many* conversion experiences. Some of these are sacramental and others may be informal steps of faith that are best and often only identified by hindsight—looking back and recognizing God's loving presence in our lives (Kimball 44–58).

All ministry is invitation. Evangelization describes the process in which we invite persons into deeper relationships with us, with themselves and with God. Jesus called for profound changes in people's lives and lifestyles, their understandings of God, of themselves and their neighbors. Jesus entered people's lives to proclaim the Reign of God, turning upside down the world order and declaring as valuable and blessed most of what the world rejects and scorns—the poor, the powerless, the grieving and the sinful. Embracing the love of God and the values preached by Jesus radically transformed people's lives, freeing them to love in previously unimagined ways. Their burdens became light, and their enemies became friends as their distant God became Abba. Their very lives became Good News. They did not have to read the Gospel, they were the Gospel. The same is true today. Ministry is ultimately the invitation to embrace God's transforming love into our lives. In youth ministry we invite young people to recognize their own goodness and see God at work in their lives and relationships.

The basic Gospel message that calls forth those moments of recognition and conversion could be structured as follows:

A. The Identity and Nature of God. Mistaken images of God must be replaced with images of a compassionate God who loves uncondi tionally. Young people are introduced to God through the story of the incarnation, Jesus' life and ministry.

B. The Good News: Healing our Humanity. Honest examination of our humanity reveals how our failures, fears and negativity prevents us from being the person God made us to be. A relational concept of sin, forgiveness and healing is essential to understand and embrace God's love.

C. The Message and Ministry of Jesus. To embrace God's love as proclaimed and lived by Jesus is to accept the values that Jesus taught. Believing Jesus' message that "the Reign of God is at hand" involves a personal decision to live the values expressed in the Sermon on the Mount (Matthew 5–7).[2]

D. Commitment to the Journey of Faith. Living the Christian lifestyle demands commitment and discipline. Maturing in one's faith requires personal risks, prayer, sacrifice and service to others, bearing fruit in the believers life and relationships.

Critical questions for conversion include:

- What have been your conversion experiences?
- What led to these experiences and what sparked them?
- Who are the people in your life who "gave you faith?
- What kind of conversions do you sparks in others' lives?
- How do you accept change in your life?

IMPLICATIONS FOR YOUTH MINISTRY

There are several important implications for our ministry with youth and for the church-at-large.

First, evangelization efforts must be connected with quality catechesis of youth so that the faith growth initiated through evangelization does not stagnate and die (Zanzig 33). Those who evangelize youth must be concerned with what catechetical efforts precede their ministry, which means staying informed and perhaps involved in junior high ministry and catechesis. As Confirmation programs increasing move into high school years, our evangelization efforts must be in concert with the Confirmation programs so that young people experience a unified approach to their faith growth.

Second, the job descriptions of all Coordinators of Youth Ministry, paid and volunteer, should include responsibility for directing or coordinating the youth outreach and evangelization efforts of the parish (or Catholic high school). There are few parishes that can hire a youth minister for evangelization only, but I believe that parishes can begin to expect youth minister and coordinators to be knowledgeable enough to direct or coordinate evangelization efforts in a parish. This would involve shared agreement on reasonable expectations and accountability.

Third, youth ministry training programs and curriculum need to show more attention to outreach and evangelization skills and processes. This means advocacy and support from leaders in the field, especially as we evaluate the recent graduates from youth ministry training programs. Johannes Hofinger lists the following as the main qualities of true evangelist: great fidelity, evangelical joy, ability to communicate the Gospel, mature faith, proper integration and collaboration (108–114). One training program cannot guarantee all these qualities, but youth ministry must give attention to systematic methods of formation in these qualities and competencies for evangelization.

Fourth, these principles of evangelization can and should be applied to the adult world, both within our youth ministry and with the greater adult community. The same tools for initiating and building relationships apply with staff, volunteers, boards, councils, and parents. If these above principles are indeed sound ministry, they will provide mutual support for all the ministries of the Church.

IMPLICATIONS FOR THE MINISTER

Christianity first became meaningful to me during high school within a Young Life Club. Hearing the stories of Jesus and how they related to my life was the spark that drew me into youth ministry. Similar experiences of people freely sharing how God has touched and changed their lives have been a continually rejuvenating force in my ministry. It is this personal proclamation of the Gospel that is the most dynamic form of evangelization and therefore, the primary energizing force in all ministry. A unique power is released during this experience that is the power of the Holy Spirit, whose job it is to energize and unify all who give their lives to God. This proclamation may be the story of a dramatic conversion moment or a gradual maturing experience, but every proclamation of the Gospel involves changed lives.

The hallmark of Jesus' ministry, the story of the early Church, the lives of the saints and successful ministry today all share the common element of lives changed by God. A common pitfall in youth ministry is to "do better ministry with youth than we do with each other." We often neglect to offer each other that which renews and inspires us the most—the stories of how God is working in our lives and ministries. We must be true to what we profess: that God lives and loves and changes our lives! The strength and credibility of youth ministers and religious educators depends upon our ability to initiate, coordinate and inspire a comprehensive youth ministry within which young people grow in mature faith within and beyond our communities. Without neglecting the importance of management skills, catechetical knowledge or organizational tools, we recognize the power that a changed life how to energize our ministry and call us deeper into our profession.

A. Proclamation Brings Passion

One friend of mine has described ministry as "that stirring in my gut and knowing that I can stir others." Is not the source of that stirring, that passion, the simple proclamation of the Good News? It is this passion that is deeper than mere feelings that come and go with each retreat. The passion is the power of God's love anchored within us. Out of this passion for God comes compassion for people. This compassion is the energy that inspires us to love the unlovable like Jesus did. Only God has infinite passion. We need our passion revived and renewed in order to continue being compassionate. We, as youth ministers, need to gather in settings which offer each other the most energizing experiences of our lives and ministries. I am not referring to fancy preaching or theologizing or "born again" stories, although all of those elements may be present. My hunger is for real life stories of how a young person's life was changed because of youth ministry or how another youth minister's life was changed by a young person's faith.

B. Telling Our Story

We each carry around a wealth of stories within us, but how do we uncover that precious wealth of Gospel within us? The following questions may call forth memories and stories from your life and ministry:

- Describe one young person who has changed or was deeply affected by your ministry. How do you see God working in that relationship?

- Which Scripture passage or image best describes youth ministry?
- How is your life different because of your belief in God?
- Who invited you into ministry? What in their life attracted you to ministry? Is that quality in evidence in your life today?
- When have you felt that you were an "instrument" of God?
- What young person (or adult) has challenged you the most? Who has been hardest to love? How have you succeeded or failed? How have you grown because of this relationship? What does God want for this relationship?
- What has been the highpoint of your ministry? What has been your greatest "success"? How do you define success in ministry?
- Describe the most meaningful "dying-rising" experience of your ministry. What or who kept you moving through it, believing in the resurrection?
- Describe the most profound prayer experience you have had with young people. What were the circumstances, your feelings, the youth's response? How has it changed you?

Our own stories may seem insignificant to us, but they are part of the Good News that nurtures our spirits. Our ministry appears as a small mustard seed and as meager as the widow's mite. Given as a gift to other ministers, our story becomes Gospel, and multiplies as the seed on good ground that bears hundredfold. The key to youth ministry is contained in the simple yet profound formula that John Shea offers: "Gather the folks, break the bread and tell the story."

A PROCESS FOR EVANGELIZING YOUTH

Part I: The Two Movements in the Evangelization Process

There are two essential movements in the evangelization process: invitation into relationship and proclamation of the Gospel. Invitation can happen in one-to-one relationships or in structured group meetings. In either case, the invitation must be personal and build a sense of community, within which the Gospel can be proclaimed. This proclamation, a sharing of faith, can either be indirect—for example, a caring friendship that communicates concern for another person—or direct, through verbal sharing of faith stories. This section of my essay examines how to apply the evangelizing style of ministry described above.

Movement 1: Invitation into Relationship

The first movement in evangelization is concerned primarily with building relationships within which faith can be shared. If an Incarnational style of ministry can be seen as being "friend-makers for God," then the following strategies will outline some practical ways of reaching out to the world of adolescents in order to communicate in ways they readily understand.

1) Tune Into Youth Culture

Get to know their world! Listen to some of their music, ask them to bring music to your groups when appropriate. Identify the TV shows, movies, rock videos, music, and magazines that express the language, thoughts, values, concerns and issues of youth. Make an attempts to get to know something about their schools, teachers, families, and interests.

2) Identify the Dynamics of the Group

When you are with a large group of young people, be sensitive to the different smaller groups represented; the schools, classes, sexes, cliques. Acknowledge these differences and challenge the whole group to build bridges between the competing groups.

3) Make Your Space Inviting

Since youth have often been in school all day, your meeting space should have a different look and feel. Private homes afford informality. If you are locked into a church setting, do your best to make your meeting space different from a classroom. Use posters, candles, music, indirect lighting, bean-bag chairs, or pillows. use anything else that will de-institutionalize your room. Make it comfortable for kids.

4) Connect Before and After the Meeting

Be prepared, so you can mix with your group before the meetings begin. After the meeting, try to connect with anyone who wants to talk seriously or just to make small talk. Much can be communicated in the informal talk before and after an event. If possible, touch base with your group members between meetings. Break down the boundary of relating only within the "program". Phone calls, Christmas or birthday cards, attendance at one of their games or concerts all can mean a great deal to young people.

5) Think in Terms of Relationships

Jim Rayburn, the founder of Young Life, had a marvelous phrase to describe this first movement of evangelization. He said, "Win the right to be heard." There are few adults willing to offer the time it takes to build a friendship with a teenager. Adolescents need the maturity and stability of adults. Many, though, attempt to move away from adult authorities in order to establish themselves, to take on an identity. Building relationship with a young person takes investments of time, concern and patience. In personally getting to know the youth in your group, you create the best context for faith-sharing. Understanding and trust are essential. What you proclaim to youth will take root as your relationships with them deepen.

Movement 2: Proclamation of the Gospel

The Gospel is best proclaimed and heard when the one proclaiming has intentionally strengthened the network of relationships in his or her community. Such a community may be as small as two persons or as large as a youth group of 50 or more adolescents. We have the power to proclaim the Gospel non-verbally, in the ways we treat young people and others. I recall one of my ministry friends, named Jack, visiting a college study who was once very active in his group. Jack wanted to know what had worked in his ministry, and why this young woman had such deep beliefs. "Was it the large group meetings, the Bible studies, the retreats, any particular talk that I gave?" Jack kept asking her. "No, none of those, although they were all great. I think that I believe in God so much because of the way you love your wife so much," she replied.

Jack's ministry programs surely had an impact on this young woman. Yet, his personal witness had the most lasting effect on her life. We proclaim the Good News when we respect young people, listen to them, care about them whether or not they regularly attend our programs. I suspect that Jesus' non-verbal communication was as rich and powerful as all the words that Gospel writers put on paper. The quality of our caring validates the truth of the Message.

The most direct way to evangelize, to share the Good News, is to tell Gospel stories. Storytelling is a traditional way by which we pass on religious faith from one generation to the next. Before the Hebrew Scriptures or the Gospels were written, read, and studied, there were oral stories, faithfully told from memory, often at meals and times of prayer. The power of stories to captivate, teach, and inspire is just as strong today as in ages past.

The best teachers, preachers, and even entertainers are those who share stories, especially their personal stories. The most precious times that we spend with family, friends, lovers, and even work associates are ones in which we exchange stories. The Hawaiian people use the phrase "to talk story" to refer to sharing one's life with someone else, to draw close, to be intimate with another.

There is a certain magic about stories. Everyone has experienced the calm, attentive mood that descends upon a group when they hear the words, "Once upon a time . . . " Listeners become like children, in the best sense of the word—open, accepting, believing, trusting. Jesus told us that we must become like little children if we are to enter the Kingdom of God (Luke 19:17). Adolescents usually have a hard time identifying with this, since they are trying to escape childhood. But storytelling and listening give youth permission to be appropriately childlike. They show more respect, often are less inhibited, and participate in a refreshingly honest way when telling or responding to a real-life story.

The Gospels include stories Jesus told and ones told about him. He taught people through stories. He was a masterful storyteller, drawing from people's lives to teach them about God's incredible love. With farmers, he talked about sewing seeds. With shepherds, he spoke of sheep. With businessmen and tax-collectors, he spoke of investing money and profits. He talked of travelers, disobedient sons, trees, pearls, wine, fishing, warfare, and other things that were part of his listeners' experiences. When people heard the rich being compared to a camel squeezing through the eye of a needle, they laughed out loud. When they heard Jesus weave the tale of a loving father embracing his sinful son, they wept. Jesus touched their humanity. He revealed Divinity. Our task is the same.

Part II: How to Design an Evangelizing Session for Youth

An effective evangelizing group session for Catholic youth contains four essential elements:

Element 1: Welcome

Always greet each young person prior to the meeting. Mix with your participants. Stay away from the spot from which you will lead the session, for example, mix with them outside the classroom, standing up, or circulating in the room. Enjoy small talk and ask them about their week. Try to make contact with each young person before beginning of every evangelizing session.

Element 2: Warm-Up and Community Building

This includes those gathering activities you will use to help youth feel safe and comfortable and to build community in the group. When a group to be evangelized is new, a significant portion of its meetings are devoted to comfort-setting. An opening prayer and introduction to the session are also included during Warm-Up time.

Element 3: The "Work" of the Session: Presenting the Story of Faith

"Work" here refers to the main purpose of a youth evangelization session. It can include storytelling, Scripture proclamation and reading, reflection talks, witness talks, small-group activities, and personal goal-setting. During this phase of youth evangelization meetings, participants hear and reflect on Bible stories, discover how the Christian story relates to their own stories, and dialogue with each other (and with trusted adult evangelizers) on what they are discovering.

Element 4: Wrap-Up

Wrap-Up generally includes a summary of what has happened during a session, highlighting the most important aspects of the evangelizing experience. Closing prayer(s) and pinpointing of Scripture passages for follow-up reflection and study should also take place during the Wrap-Up phase of a session.

A Session Outline

Ninety minutes is the typical duration for a youth evangelization session such as this. This estimate is based on work with an average size group, about 10–25 young people. However, the actual length of any evangelizing activity will depend on a number of variables—the number of youth in your group, their ages and maturity levels, their willingness to fully participate in the discussions and activities, and the setting for your meetings and its limitations. Each session should include a socializing time, a natural element in the process of youth evangelization. If the total time needed for an individual session is estimated to be less than 90 minutes, you could devote a substantial time to socializing. Should you require only sixty or seventy minutes for your evangelizing session, conclude the formal part of your meeting and move on to relaxed and structured time for building and deepening relationships within your group.

1. Welcome and Greeting of Participants

2. Warm-Up and Community Building

Suggested: Community-building activities, icebreakers, non-competitive games, jokes, live music with sing-a-long opportunities, recorded popular music, Christian rock music, skits, charades; incorporate an opening prayer.

3. The "Work" of the Session: Presenting the Story of Faith

a. A brief presentation, based on a story from the speaker's own life. (This storyteller/speaker can be an adult leader or a youth leader in the group.)

Suggested: The main points of the personal story and experiences described in this talk should relate directly to the main point(s) of the Scripture story to be told later in the session. This presentation of a personal story from the speaker's own life should incorporate humor, questions, irony (if possible), and reflections on an experience with which most listeners can easily identify (for example: being young and awkward; fearing rejection; feeling cared about by someone).

b. Presentation of a Bible story, by the same speaker/storyteller.

Suggested: Try to make the Scripture "come alive," bring it up-to-date by placing the characters and events in contemporary settings (for example: at the shopping mall; at school; in situations of stress or entertainment). Describe the characters well—name their feelings, how they look, what they wear, what is on their minds. Try to get listeners to empathize with these Bible figures. Use humor, suspense, surprise, and paradox when feasible.

c. A brief, personal reflection, by the same storyteller/speaker on the meaning of the Bible story and how God or Jesus Christ speaks to us through it.

Suggested: State the main point(s) of the Bible story clearly, succinctly. Use only one phrase or one sentence to point out each major point. The speaker here should witness to all participants what the Scripture story means to him or her, how God calls to us or challenges us in the passage, and how the participants could apply the message(s) and main point(s) of the Scripture story to their own lives, were they to take it to heart.

d. Option: Opportunities for group discussion, storytelling among participants, small-group activities, quiet reflection time, artistic responses, and so forth.

Suggested: In helping youth-being-evangelized to apply the Scripture and personal stories told to their lives, provide one or two reflection activities, or perhaps one reflection-discussion activity and, if group members are mature enough, one quiet-time period to let it all soak in. You also might consider giving participants a chance to now tell their own personal stories which relate to the Scripture being proclaimed.

4. Wrap-Up and Closing Prayer (Option: Social Time/Refreshments)

Suggested: Summarize some of the key aspects of the youth evangelization session which has just taken place. Group leader and/or main speaker should make verbal note of key contributions and insights by participants too. Identify a few Scripture passages for further reflection and study during the coming week or two. Offer participants the chance to set an action step for themselves, as a result of the Scripture proclaimed and stories shared. (Note: in an action step, a participant identifies what his or her concrete response-in-faith to the Gospel will be in the immediate future.) Close with prayer, reflective music—live or recorded, sing-a-long music, humor or jokes, announcements. Social time and refreshments should follow whenever possible.

CONCLUSION

"What are you doing here." Linda asked

"Oh, I'm here to see old friends and make some new ones," I replied. I had gotten to know this assertive sophomore hanging out in the music room at Apollo High. I grew accustomed to that question from most of the kids I met there, but was unprepared for the new one.

"Do you have a job?"

"Why, yes." I said, taking a breath and explained that four churches were paying for me to do youth work. She had grown to like me and was somewhat dismayed that such a nice guy was involved with a church, but asked one more question to satisfy her curiosity.

"Which ones?" she asked skeptically, only to be surprised to find that her church was one of my sponsors. It did not get her any more involved with church at that point in her life, but certainly changed her image of the Church.

I hope that we in youth ministry keep surprising kids, not just with zany skits and bad jokes, but catch them off guard by showing up on their turf, without roles or rules to restrict our relationships with them. I hope we surprise them by calling them by name, as Jesus did to Zacchaeus. I hope our vulnerability quietly disarms them of their defenses. I hope our faith and lifestyle creates curiosity among the young, a curiosity that leads them to track down the source of the love they experience in our presence.

All of our evangelizing will be energized by the holiest of surprises— the incarnation. We will be energized by the God who came in weakness and left in glory, who shows up on our doorstep to invite us to the eternal banquet of love, whose Spirit is at home in our flesh, who bids us to bring this Good News to young people.

> Go, therefore, make disciples of all nations; baptize them in the name of the Father and of the Son and of the Holy Spirit, and teach them to observe all the commands I gave you. And know that I am with you always; yes, to the end of time (Matthew 28: 19–20, *Jerusalem Bible*).

End Notes

[1] For more information on Young Life Ministry see Jeffrey Johnson and Char Meredith below.

[2] For excellent theology and practical examples of how to retell the story of Jesus, see John Shea below. His stories illustrate how to draw the religious meaning of people's lives without imposing a spirituality on them.

Works Cited

The Challenge of Adolescent Catechesis. Washington, DC: NFCYM, 1986.

Hater, Robert. *The Relationship Between Evangelization and Catechesis*. Washington, DC: NCDD Publications, 1981.

Hofinger, SJ, Johannes. *Evangelization and Catechesis*. New York: Paulist Press, 1976.

Johnson, Jeff. "Young Life Ministry: Room for Catholic Youth Ministers." *Resources for Youth Ministry*. Ed. Michael Warren. New York: Paulist Press, 1978. 45–58.

Kimball, Don. *Power and Presence: A Theology of Relationships*. San Francisco: Harper and Row, 1986.

Meredith, Char. *It's a Sin to Bore a Kid*. Waco, TX: Word Books, 1978.

Nelson, James B. *Between Two Gardens: Reflections on Sexuality and Religious Experience*. New York: Pilgrim Press, 1983. 16–29.

Nouwen, Henri. *Reaching Out*. Garden City, NY: Doubleday, 1975.

O'Connor, Elizabeth. *The Eighth Day of Creation: Gifts and Creativity*. Waco, TX: Word Books, 1971.

Pope Paul VI. *On Evangelization in the Modern World* [*Evangelii Nuntiandi*]. Washington, DC: USCC, 1976.

Sharing the Light of Faith. NCCB. Washington, DC: USCC, 1979.

Shea, John. *Stories of Faith*. Chicago: Thomas More Press, 1983.

Shea, John. *An Experience Named Spirit*. Chicago: Thomas More Press, 1983.

Shea, John. *Spirit Master*. Chicago: Thomas More Press, 1987.

A Vision of Youth Ministry. Department of Education. Washington, DC: USCC, 1976.

Warren, Michael. "Catechesis for the 1980's." *Youth and the Future of the Church*. New York: Seabury Press, 1982.

Zanzig, Tom. *Sharing Manual*. Winona, MN: St. Mary's Press, 1985.

CHAPTER 7

INTEGRATING EVANGELIZATION STRATEGIES INTO THE COMPONENTS OF A COMPREHENSIVE YOUTH MINISTRY

REYNOLDS R. EKSTROM
AND
JOHN ROBERTO

Evangelization cannot be packaged into a neat program. It is first and foremost an attitude, a commitment, even a fervor, that becomes the energizing core of our ministry efforts with young people. The proclamation of the Good News is most effective when integrated into a comprehensive approach to youth ministry. A Vision of Youth Ministry *provides a framework for developing this approach to ministry with young people.*

The components of a holistic youth ministry, as described in the Vision *document, are interdependent. When viewed through a single lens, they provide a complete picture of Catholic youth ministry's field of action. Naturally, the youth ministry agenda and goals will vary from place to place, depending on the needs and resources in each unique local situation. However, there are many creative ways in which local parishes, schools and other faith communities evangelize young people through the components of youth ministry.*

—The Challenge of Catholic Youth Evangelization

IN THE DOCUMENT, *The Challenge of Catholic Youth Evangelization*, we are reminded that evangelization "cannot be packaged" into a concise, neat, "one size fits all" youth program (*Challenge* 19). The *Challenge* maintains that evangelization, in fact, is "first and foremost an attitude, a commitment, even a fervor that becomes the energizing core" of our various ministries with young people. It goes on to add that the proclamation of the Good News is most effective when it is integrated into a comprehensive approach to youth ministry.

Of course, the foundational, blueprint paper, *A Vision of Youth Ministry*, published in 1976, was the first practical resource to provide a framework, for local Catholic communities, on how to develop a holistic, or comprehensive, approach to ministry with adolescents. Since the publication of the *Vision* paper (USCC 1976)—with the recent support of the new *Challenge* document—a Catholic vision of holistic youth ministry has spoken consistently of components to a holistic youth ministry which are separate, distinguishable, but *interdependent*. When viewed through a "single lens," as the *Challenge* points out, these separate but interdependent components of an overall ministry provide a complete picture of Catholic youth ministry's field of action. Naturally, the youth ministry agenda will vary from place to place, depending on the needs and resources in each unique, local situation. However, there are many creative ways in which local parishes, schools and other faith communities evangelize young people through the components of youth ministry (*Challenge* 19).

In this way, then, the Church's outreach to youth, over the past twenty years or so, has entered a "new day" and has traveled many "new roads." Many young people and adults, in grass-roots communities, have been "experimenting with and creating new forms of pastoral ministry" which genuinely seeks to evangelize adolescents and challenge them to Christian conversion and lifestyles (*Vision* 2) These new forms of ministry, dedicated to the pastoral care of youth, do not always look like neatly packaged, one size for all youth programs. What they often inspire is a longing to share faith with the young, in a variety of ways, schedules and formats, and ministry teams, which all strive—in Christian unity and commitment—to evangelize young people (i.e., to introduce young people to Jesus and the community which follows him) with an urgency unseen in times recently gone by.

In this chapter, we will try to describe the nature of a comprehensive youth ministry, outline characteristics of the *interdependent* components of a comprehensive youth ministry, indicate a number of ways by which adolescents can be evangelized, intentionally, through these components, and note special considerations to keep in mind whenever one undertakes a personal, evangelizing approach to outreach in the name of the Lord. In doing so, we hope—in conjunction with those who formed *The Challenge of Catholic Youth Evangelization* statement—that our ideas will cause your local team members and you to engage in "an honest examination of (your) current approach to the evangelization of young people...the first task of those responsible for the faith community's ministry to young people in all settings: parish, school, community, diocese, and other youth-serving organizations and programs" (*Challenge* 25).

A COMPREHENSIVE, EVANGELIZING YOUTH MINISTRY

Grounded in the Evangelizing Mission of Jesus and the Church

The mission of the Church is also the mission of youth ministry. Youth ministry is one of the ministries of the Church and therefore participates in realizing the evangelizing mission of the Church with youth.

> As one among many ministries of the Church, youth ministry must be understood in terms of the mission and ministry of the whole Church . . . The Church's mission is threefold: to proclaim the good news of salvation, offer itself as a group of people transformed by the Spirit into a community of faith, hope, and love; and to bring God's justice and love to others through service in its individual, social, and political dimensions (*Vision* 3).

Far from peripheral to the Church's concern, youth ministry is *essential* for helping the Church realize its mission with its young members. In this light, you could say that *youth ministry means becoming Church with young people*—focusing the ministries of the Church upon this unique stage of life with its distinct life tasks and social context *and* then actively engaging young people as disciples in the mission of Jesus Christ and the Church.

This threefold mission of the Church, rooted in the reign of God, as proclaimed by Jesus, forms the basis for the goals and the framework or components of youth ministry: *Word* (Evangelization and Catechesis), *Prayer and Worship, Community Life, Justice and Service, Pastoral Care* (Guidance and Healing), *Leadership Development* (Enablement), and *Advocacy*. The correlation between the components of youth ministry and the mission of the Church is unmistakable:

Mission of the Church	Corresponding Component of Youth Ministry
Proclamation of the Gospel in *word* and in *sacrament*, in an *organized* and *authorized* manner.	Evangelization Catechesis Prayer and Worship
Proclamation of the Gospel by the *quality* of the *Church's own life*	Community Life Guidance/Pastoral Care
Proclamation of the Gospel by *application* of the Gospel to the struggle for *social justice, peace,* and *human rights* (*Catholicism* 717)	Justice and Service Advocacy

Situating youth ministry within the evangelizing mission of the Church necessitates developing a communal model of youth ministry which adequately addresses the scope of the Church's evangelizing mission. A youth ministry should look and act like the (ideal) parish community, but in microcosm. To be effective, ministry with youth seeks to achieve a balance among the many components of a comprehensive ministry. Each of these components revolves around the community's own life. Seen from this angle, youth ministry operates out of the community's life.

The components of a comprehensive, communal youth ministry give shape and direction to the Church's goal of adolescent evangelization. Briefly, these components are:

■ **Advocacy**: *interpreting* the needs of youth and their families, especially the social problems facing them and *acting* with or on behalf of youth and their families for a change in the systems (policies, procedures, programs) which create or contribute to the social problems; *giving* young people a voice and *empowering* them to address the social problems that they face.

■ **Catechesis**: *sponsoring* youth toward maturity in Catholic Christian faith as a living reality through the kind of teaching and learning that emphasizes understanding, reflection, and transformation; *fostering* in youth a communal identity as Catholic Christians within the intergenerational community of faith *and* helping them to develop their own personal faith identity.

■ **Community Life**: *creating* an environment which nurtures meaningful relationships among youth and between youth and adults characterized by Gospel values (e.g. acceptance of all people, trust, respect, cooperation, honesty, taking responsibility, willingness to serve); *helping* young people feel like a valued part of the church community; *providing* opportunities for social interaction and meaningful participation in the life of the church and civic community.

■ **Evangelization**: *proclaiming* through word and witness the Good News of the Gospel to youth who have not yet heard or seen it and *inviting* them into a relationship with Jesus Christ and the community of believers; *ongoing witness* of the faith community as it attempts to live out the Gospel with such authenticity that the faith of all the members is sustained and nourished. Evangelization is the energizing core of all the components of youth ministry.

■ **Justice, Peace, and Service**: *guiding* young people in the development of a social consciousness and a commitment to a life of justice and service grounded in their faith in Jesus Christ, in the scriptures and in Catholic social teaching; *empowering* young people (and their families) to work for justice by concrete efforts to address the causes of human suffering, to serve those in need, to pursue peace, and to defend the life, dignity, and rights of all people; *infusing* the concepts of justice and peace into all youth ministry efforts.

■ **Leadership Development/Enablement**: *recruiting, training,* and *supporting* youth and adult leaders in youth ministry; *empowering* youth for leadership and ministry with their peers, in their schools, and in the church and civic community; *developing* a leadership team of youth and adults to organize and coordinate a ministry with youth; *partnering* with parents and families in promoting positive youth development and faith growth.

■ **Pastoral Care/Guidance**: *promoting* positive youth and family development through a variety of preventive strategies (e.g., developing life skills and parenting skills); *caring* for youth and families in crisis through support, counseling, and referral to appropriate community agencies; and *providing* guidance as youth face life decisions and make moral choices.

■ **Prayer and Worship**: *assisting* young people in deepening their relationship with Jesus through spiritual development and a personal prayer life; *providing* a variety of communal prayer and worship experiences with youth to deepen and celebrate their relationship with Jesus in a caring Christian community; *involving* young people in the sacramental life of the Church.

EXPRESSED CREATIVELY THROUGH INTERDEPENDENT MINISTRY ACTIVITIES

Ministry of Advocacy

The document, *The Challenge of Catholic Youth Evangelization* notes that all persons interested in the needs of adolescents today "are called to advocate" for them by taking "the initiative in raising the faith community's consciousness of (its) responsibility to young people" (*Challenge* 21). It adds:

> The faith community must be made fully aware of its duty to be inviting and welcoming to young people. The faith community should also be challenged to enable the meaningful participation of adolescents and their families in the mission and ministry of the church. The secular community must be challenged to respond adequately to youths' needs and to enable young people to use their gifts and talents for the good of others (*Challenge* 21).

Practically speaking, how do we evangelize adolescents today through a ministry of Christian advocacy? Consider some of the following pastoral steps now being taken in various church congregations around the country:

- Adults remind the faith community as a whole and leadership groups/structures (e.g., parish council, finance committees), in particular, of the community's evangelizing responsibility to welcome and involve all youth as full members of the people of God;
- Advocacy for adequate staff, facilities, and resources for comprehensive, culturally-appropriate evangelizing ministries;
- Give witness, to all in the faith community, about the presence of God in the lives of young people and to speak up on behalf of the various needs of youth whenever and wherever necessary;
- Give adolescents a voice in the local faith community (in its ministries, deliberations, and decisions) and empower young people to address the faith issues and social concerns in their lives.

Ministry of Catechesis

The Challenge of Catholic Youth Evangelization speaks of catechesis as "a vital expression of the ministry of the Word" (*Challenge* 19). Evangelization and catechesis ministries are intimately related. In fact, as has so often been pointed out, the desire to proclaim the gospel of Jesus is at the heart of adolescent catechesis (*CT* 19). *The Challenge* document notes clearly:

> Effective programs of adolescent catechesis are vital in strengthening and deepening young people's response to the proclamation of the Good News. These opportunities build upon the initial phases of evangelization—Christian witness, outreach, proclamation . . . by explaining gospel truths fully and enthusiastically. Therefore, catechesis flows from and enhances foundational evangelizing activities (*Challenge* 19).

Practically speaking, how do we evangelize adolescents through a ministry of catechesis? Consider the following ways:

- Catechists, DREs, and support staff give authentic Christian witness in their work with young people and in all aspects of their lives;
- Through Scripture-sharing, storytelling activities, and various types of catechetical sessions/activities, young people are challenged to hear God's Word and to apply the Good News to their life questions and experiences;
- Through systematic and culturally-appropriate catechetical models, young people are challenged to mature, in the image of Jesus, as persons and as member of the wider faith community.

Ministry of Community-Building

Young people should sense that they are welcome in their home parishes and school faith communities. They should sense, equally, that those they encounter in these places are interested in evangelizing them, in order to nurture them in Christian faith. A local community nurtures the budding faith of young men and women through its people, people who "embrace" adolescents in Christ by their own Christian witness, outreach, hospitality, welcoming attitudes, and other forms of basic pastoral care. *The Challenge of Catholic Youth Evangelization* has much to say on this matter.

A community of believers best enables young people to experience the Good News by nurturing a sense of belonging and acceptance, a sense of "being home" in the parish, in the diocese,
and in the universal church (*Challenge* 20).

In practical terms, how does the faith community evangelize its young
members through a ministry of welcome, friendship, and community-building? Here are some ministry efforts being implemented in places throughout the country.

■ Through person-to-person outreach and friendship-development:
youth to youth, and adult-to-youth;
■ Helping young people feel valued and wanted in the community;
■ Providing adolescents chances for meaningful social interaction and
participation in various activities within the faith community and
throughout the wider community;
■ Through social gatherings and group-building celebrations, rooted in
a gospel spirit of hospitality, on occasions throughout the year;
■ Through intergenerational and family-centered experiences to which
all adolescents, their parents, and other family members are cor-
dially invited;
■ Making it possible for our youth-oriented groups/activities to become more inclusive or all young people—especially those who
are poor, alienated, newcomers, and members of various ethnic and
cultural groups.

Ministry of Justice and Service

The fundamental mission of each person who follows Jesus is to reach
out, in his name, to become a sign of hope and a witness to the reign of
God. In the landmark document, *A Vision of Youth Ministry*, a number of
things were said, pertaining to the mission of evangelization and justice
and service with adolescents. The *Vision* claimed:

The justice and service aspect of youth ministry is based on the
responsibility of the Church to extend the kingdom of God in
the world . . . As the bishops affirmed in (their) landmark statement, *Justice in the World,* "Action on behalf of justice and participation in the transformation of the world appear to us as a
constitutive dimension of the preaching of the Gospel" (18).

Therefore, the *Vision* document noted, a ministry component which focuses youth—and the entire faith community—on service and action(s) on behalf of justice "should be constitutive dimensions" of the church's overall, evangelizing ministry for adolescents. A balanced picture, in a local parish or school situation, will emphasize several things.

> First of all, by exercising moral leadership and sharing its material and human resources, the Church in ministry with youth must live out a commitment to young people and communities who suffer discrimination, poverty, handicaps, and injustice. Second, by providing models, experiences, and programs, the faith community . . . should fulfill its responsibility to educate youth for justice and to call young people themselves to action on behalf of others (18).

Well-balanced ministry programs/activities which involve social action, critical Christian reflection, and justice education evangelize adolescents and enable their growth into maturing, self-giving followers of the Lord (*Vision* 19). As they hear the gospel and as they are challenged toward Christian discipleship, adolescents in local parishes, schools, and other settings, should be encouraged to "put their gifts, skills, and talents at the service of God's human family and all the world" (*Challenge* 20). Earlier in this chapter, we noted that this can be done in a number of ways, in the 1990s, wherever a comprehensive approach to youth evangelization is being implemented:

- by guiding youth toward social consciousness and commitment to a life of justice and service, grounded in the gospel's vision and values and grounded in Catholic social teaching;
- by empowering young men and women (and their family members) to work for justice, through concrete efforts to address human suffering, to serve those in need, to pursue peace, and to defend the life and rights of all human beings;
- by infusing justice and peace concepts into all youth ministry efforts on all levels;
- by "partnering" with parents and other family members in an attempt to promote healthy adolescent development, Christian faith growth, and just and socially-concerned lifestyles in adolescents' households.

There are other means, today, by which we can integrate and promote Christian justice and service awareness in the broad endeavor to evangelize young people. In fact, at this time, some ministry programs are attempting at least some of the following:

- Cultural immersion experiences;
- Regularly scheduled justice education programs and group activities;
- Regularly scheduled and supported Christian service projects for both adolescents and their family members.

Ministry of Leadership Development (Enablement)

The Challenge of Catholic Youth Evangelization makes special note of the fact that those in youth ministry have a responsibility "to foster the gifts, talents, and skills of young people and provide opportunities" for adolescents to use them in the local faith community and in the wider society (*Challenge* 21). It adds:

> Enablement (of youth) present opportunities for evangelization when young people themselves become evangelizers. Adolescents themselves are called to share the Good News in witness and in Word. For young people, there is no more powerful witness than other young people's own stories of the presence of God in their lives (*Challenge* 21).

How do we typically prepare adolescents, today, for their own ministries of evangelization and their own work as peer witnesses? Consider some of the following possibilities:

- Development of leadership teams of youth and adults to organize and coordinate the local evangelizing, comprehensive ministry to and for young people;
- Development of a "partnership" with parents and the other members of adolescents' families in order to promote lifestyles rooted in the gospel's vision and values in the actual households of young people;
- Leadership training for young people in the skills of Christian outreach, faith-sharing, storytelling, Bible use, Scripture proclamation, and public speaking;
- Education for peer evangelizers on how to prepare prayer experiences and worship rituals for others.

Ministry of Pastoral Care (Guidance)

The aspect of a comprehensive youth evangelization model known as pastoral care presents many opportunities for sharing good news and the healing touch of the Lord with young people. *The Challenge of Catholic Youth Evangelization* has stressed that pastoral care, in a sense, "involves personal, spiritual, and vocational guidance" offered to the young (*Challenge* 20). It affirms that many adolescents, in our day, experience pain, hurt, alienation, and questions and concerns that seem bigger than life itself. In evangelizing young people through moments of personal guidance and pastoral outreach, youth's evangelizers

> provide opportunities for young people's holistic growth, family outreach, and information on critical issues facing young people. Experiences of woundedness provide a natural entry point for the healing power of God. Often, in the midst of such experiences, young people are most open to the liberating and freeing message of the gospel (*Challenge* 20–21).

Those involved in comprehensive youth ministries report a number of means now being explored as ways to care pastorally for youth in need of "good news," any good news, including the healing touch of their God. Some of these include:

- Individual relationships rooted in Christian care, listening, and support;
- Ritual experiences of the sacrament of reconciliation and individual confession;
- Outreach to youth at-risk and young people in crisis;
- Promotion of Christian values through prevention programs (e.g., "Just say no . . . " programs) and through life-skills programs taught to adolescents and to their family members;
- Guidance for young people and families, on various moral issues and other matters, through counseling services, referral services, and follow-up support endeavors.

Ministry of Prayer and Worship

The Challenge of Catholic Youth Evangelization notes the decisive impact that authentic, inclusive worship can have on the Christian evangelization of the young today. It says:

In the wider faith community, young people experience the faith and prayerfulness of a celebrating church. Meaningful youth liturgies and intergenerational worship experiences include the proclamation of the Good News and the celebration of the sacraments. These experiences challenge young people to grow in faith (and) serve to nurture that growth (*Challenge* 19–20).

There are many examples which indicate how prayer and worship ministries help serve the cause of youth evangelization and fit, naturally, into the scope of a comprehensive model of youth ministry.

- Through celebration of liturgies of the Word with adolescents
- Through regular celebration of the Eucharist and the sacrament of Reconciliation with and for young people
- Through homilies that lively and relevant for adolescents
- Through the active participation, by young people themselves, in the participation of and in the celebration of each of the types of prayer named above
- Through the use of a variety of private and communal prayer forms with youth
- Through the use of "young people's symbols and music" and other important materials in Christian prayer
- Through celebration of the deepening of our personal and corporate friendship with Jesus whenever we gather to pray or otherwise attempt to grow in Christian spirituality

SPECIAL CONSIDERATIONS: PROCEED WITH CARE

In attempting to evangelize adolescents through the components of Catholic youth ministry—in other words, through a comprehensive, communal pastoral model—the challenge, of course, is immense. Yet the work must begin. And if it has not yet begun in earnest in your own local faith community, it must begin now. Perhaps you recognize, as so many now do, that a new model of youth evangelization—a comprehensive or holistic vision and model—is needed to guide Christian thinking and planning for the present generation of adolescents and their families. As you proceed, do so with care. And keep in mind a few simple but compelling pastoral guidelines, with which this chapter will close.

A comprehensive, evangelizing youth ministry must promote holistic growth for all involved.

We need a model of youth ministry that corresponds to a contemporary understanding of adolescent development and faith growth. Specifically, one that promotes the internal assets and faith life of youth, while strengthening the external, community supports for positive youth development. We need a model that attends to a wide set of youth needs and that is attuned to the distinct developmental and social needs of young and older adolescents.

A comprehensive, evangelizing youth ministry must remain family-and community-centered.

We need a model of youth ministry that moves beyond traditional youth-only programming to include ministry with families, incorporation of young people into all aspects of church life, and partnerships with other churches/synagogues, schools, and community agencies in a common effort to promote positive youth development. Youth ministry needs to situate itself within this broader context.

A comprehensive, evangelizing youth ministry must remain flexible and inclusive.

We need a model of youth ministry which responds creatively and flexibly to *all* the youth of the parish, not just the ones who attend programs. We need a model which is designed to enlarge the number of approaches and methods used to minister with youth so that all youth can be reached through a local community's youth ministry. Gone are the days when one program structure can respond to all the needs of youth.

A comprehensive, evangelizing youth ministry must always remain fundamentally and profoundly relational—it must put persons first.

We need a model of youth ministry that recognizes the changing needs and life situations of young people and their families and places this reality ahead of program structures. *Programs are made for people; people are not made for programs.* We need a flexible, adaptable model of youth ministry that can be tailored to address the real needs and life situations of today's young people and their families in particular community settings.

Above all, a comprehensive, evangelizing youth ministry must be Jesus-centered and rooted in gospel values.

We need a model of youth ministry that is well grounded in the mission and ministry of Jesus Christ and his church. We need a model which will provide a clear understanding of youth ministry as integral to the life of the church.

Works Cited

John Paul II. *Catechesi Tradendae.* Washington, DC: USCC Publishing, 1979.

National Federation for Catholic Youth Ministry. *The Challenge of Catholic Youth Evangelization.* Washington, DC: NFCYM, 1993.

A Vision of Youth Ministry. Washington, DC: USCC Publishing, 1986 Edition.

CHAPTER 8

THE EVANGELIZING COMMUNITY: PARTNERSHIPS IN THE EVANGELIZATION OF ADOLESCENTS

REYNOLDS R. EKSTROM

Who has the mission of evangelizing? By divine mandate, the duty of going out into the world and preaching the Gospel to every creature rests with the whole Church. The work of evangelization is a basic duty of the People of God. (Evangelii Nuntiandi 59).

Effective evangelization of young people, therefore, requires that an evangelizing community proclaim the Good News in a language young people understand.

—The Challenge of Catholic Youth Evangelization

THE MISSION HAS A CHURCH AND A PEOPLE

An old saying, "Values are caught not taught," comes to mind as I think about two churches I have visited in recent months.

At St. Nobody's parish, a new pastor and staff had taken over. The parish's founding pastor had died, after spending twenty years in the community drawing all power and control toward himself and a few chosen lay consultants. At Sunday liturgies, hardly a young person over 12 could be seen. The families there seemed to drag through the right Catholic motions during the rituals. However, when I asked the new pastor and staff about adolescent ministry options, as I talked with them about pastoral planning for the whole community, I was assured that youth were not a problem. Most go to Catholic high schools. And that takes care of that. Besides they had a parish CYO—for 15 youth who came to meetings regularly (there are over 1000 teenagers within this parish's boundaries), and they were considering a youth retreat for next year.

Young people were not even on the parish's radar screen. Most had disappeared, right after Confirmation, during decades of pastoral neglect. While the departed pastor had worked hard to squirrel away many thousands of dollars in parish cash reserves, human needs had often been neglected. Of course, not all the young people in St. Nobody's go to Catholic schools. Many go to public schools, significant numbers are Hispanic with Spanish as their first language, and many Anglo and Hispanic youth drop out of school before eleventh grade. In terms of sharing faith meaningfully with adolescents and their families, in this very large parish, it would be a long road back.

At St. Gospela's Church, the pastoral staff was eager to talk. They had hired a new youth outreach coordinator to do ministry with young people in the surrounding, racially-mixed neighborhoods. Every liturgy seemed like a celebration, especially when the gospel choir or youth choir led the community in song. The youth ministry staff, primarily African-American Catholics, holds weekly Bible study and other types of ministry events in the community. Some young people go to Catholic schools, but many wind up in poor-quality public education or drop out altogether. The new coordinator, an African-American, says that what he most wants is to reach out to help young people, often very poor and troubled, find a reason to believe. The staff, overall, acknowledges that they see themselves mirrored in youth and worry about the future of their community. St. Gospela's isn't perfect, but they're working at handing on the faith to all generations one step at a time.

As you look over these two vignettes, which of these parishes is doing the work of evangelization? Where should St. Nobody's staff begin? What should St. Gospela's do to enrich its approaches? What should be the goal of each community in reaching out to adolescents? Which people should each parish staff try to enlist in their evangelizing efforts and what Christian partnerships should they form?

By definition, a community is a group of individuals who share common beliefs, values, and tasks or responsibilities. All members of the worldwide Christian church community have a share in the essential mission of evangelization. Paul VI pointed this out with the words,

Who has the mission of evangelizing? By divine mandate, the duty of going out into the world and preaching the Gospel to every creature rests with the whole Church. The work of evangelization is a basic duty of (all) the people of God (EN 59).

A fundamental Christian principle affirms that our invisible, loving Creator is present to all humanity in and through the visible and material in creation, in all their "favorable as well as dangerous aspects" to use Bernard Haring's phrase (Haring 6). Some Christian assemblies today stress a spirituality "not of this world" which focuses, like a tunnel vision, on a God-and-me relationship. Yet authentic Christian expression affirms that the saving encounter between Jesus Christ and human beings "occurs not only personally and individually but corporately and ecclesially" (McBrien 900–901). Whenever we are in communion with other Christians, reaching out to others, sharing faith with them, and responsibly caring for the creation which God has given us, we are in fact in communion with Christ.

So, as members of his church, each of us has an obligation to share the Lord's good news of universal salvation—with those who have heard it before and believed as well as those who have never encountered the message. In the Gospel of Matthew, the risen Jesus tells his followers:

"Go, then, to all peoples everywhere and make them my disciples: baptize them in the name of the Father, the Son, and the Holy Spirit, and teach them to obey everything I have commanded you. And I will be with you always, to the end of the age" (Matt 28:19–20).

Such are the "profound demands of God's life within us," as John Paul II says (RM 11). The community of the one true Evangelizer is guided by his Spirit, and from that Spirit come the hope and the charisms needed to evangelize—often at the price of crucifying effort. Today, the mission has a church and a people. The deepest identity and vocation of this community is evangelization (EN 14). The aim of the mission can be summed in simple words and phrases such as, conversion, interior change of individuals and whole cultures, the reign of God. Put another way,

> the Church evangelizes when (it) seeks to convert, solely through the divine power of the message (proclaimed), both the personal and collective consciences of people, the activities in which they engage, and the lives and concrete milieu which are theirs (EN 18).

To do so effectively, community members must learn and value the languages of particular individuals and cultures, especially the unique languages of young people today, in order to proclaim the Good News well. To do so effectively, many partnerships and collaborations should be formed (in fact, the roots of the term community—*koinonia*—refer to "partnership"). And to do its evangelizing work faithfully, the Church community must also examine its own house, as it were, and become critically aware of the ways it needs to be changed and renewed from within in order to walk in the image and likeness of the one, true Evangelizer.

CHARACTERISTICS OF THE EVANGELIZING COMMUNITY

Certain characteristics mark the Christian community which strives to share faith with adolescents in meaningful ways. *The Challenge of Catholic Youth Evangelization* notes that any ministry with adolescents must of course echo, in many ways, the central message of Jesus, God's Word made flesh: repent, believe, and change your lives—the reign of God is near (*Challenge* 4). In addition, the Church's pastoral ministry becomes "good news" for young people whenever it embodies the following characteristics.

1. Welcomes them and offers them hospitality

Evangelization is much more than "words." It is rooted in hope in something not seen and a promise one dares not imagine. Evangelization is done, initially, through common, everyday words and deeds which testify to friendship with Jesus. Welcome and hospitality are special deeds which tell young people that they are cared about and that they matter. In this regard, evangelization through welcome and friendship should know no brakes and no boundaries. Evangelizers hold the One who came to serve, not to be served, and to give his all for others as their ultimate model. Through welcome and hospitality—essentially through Christian charity—ministers give themselves in order to give life and hope to the young and, in the most immediate but ordinary ways, initiate the pastoral care which will serve the totality of young people's needs.

Adolescents know intuitively whether or not they are welcome somewhere. It is a mistake to reduce concepts like welcome and hospitality to perfunctory greetings at the door or icebreaker activities. Welcome and hospitality are more a matter of pastoral style. This style should permeate the whole Christian community, particularly the styles and actions of those who reach out to the community's young members.

2. Gives living witness to the faith story

To give authentic Christian witness, a faith community must authentically live the Good News. Through its lifestyle of Christian hope and service, it must be a sign of contradiction to the wider American culture. Interestingly, George Gallup's research has pointed out that the values and lifestyles of the baptized in America do not often differ much from the values and lifestyles of those never baptized.

Paul VI called authentic witness by Christians a "silent proclamation" of the Gospel, because through the everyday words and deeds of believers a new way of life is revealed. (EN 21) What are the most outstanding signs of Christian witness which inspire young people? Naturally, they are the signs which characterize the ministry of the original Evangelizer. Signs such as concern for persons weak and suffering; lives which are lived simply, humbly, and honestly; and courageous and prophetic stands against injustices and social corruptions.

3. Truly values young people

The impulse to share the Gospel ideal with adolescents, as something to be embraced and lived, stems from our compassion for them. Imparting a sense of hope and value, compassionately, to young people is a service the Christian community renders to society as a whole. In valuing youth, we help them discover and name the Lord already active and present in the relationships, the ordinary experiences, the families, and the religious and cultural traditions which are theirs (*Challenge* 7–8). Thus, in valuing them, we encourage them to mature as persons, in the name of Christ.

Evangelizers should recognize that moments of hurt, need, alienation, and crisis are particularly significant entry points for proclamation of the Good News and the healing the Lord offers to all. With John Paul II, though, we often lament that the experience of church, for any adolescents and young adults, often seems wholly separate from the most significant moments of human experience. Many seem totally indifferent to what the Church community has to provide, or even live as if God does not exist.

To address these troubles of the human community as a whole, John Paul has said it's time to take a "giant step forward" in our faith-sharing efforts—a step called re-evangelization, which is the re-energizing of the baptized and the re-making of the fabric of the Christian community itself (into "mature ecclesial communities") so that people, youth in particular, can truly hear Good News which solves some of the riddles of their lives and which helps them uncover the gifts and potentials they personally possess by God's grace (CL 34).

Provides opportunities and places for youth to gather

It is normal to want to gather with like-minded, friendly others in welcoming, safe, and comfortable settings. In such situations, young people, who often encounter only stress and weighty expectations in the wider society, can develop friendships. They can get personal and relational needs met. They can share community and also Christian faith in many ways.

Visionary, evangelizing ministers today will acknowledge the many dehumanizations, disillusionments, disintegrations, and tempting distractions with which young people are confronted frequently in our techno-pop culture. They will know that many persons and many families feel lost and alone. They will see that the split between the Gospel and mainstream culture is one of the great dramas of our age, and one that must be addressed by Christian communities. The visionary evangelizer will picture the faith community as a place in which deep longings can be touched in caring, personal relationships. Youth outreach is of special assistance here, in that it often leads to a person-to-person evangelization and an opportunity to invite the young into safe, structured Christian gatherings.

Earlier, we spoke of a gospel value called compassion. Christian compassion reminds us to be especially mindful of those young men and women who do not have a family to belong to, literally or figuratively, for whatever reasons. They truly deserve welcoming, friendly, safe places to gather in Jesus' name. John Paul II has noted:

> There exist in the world countless people who unfortunately cannot in any sense claim membership in what could be called in the proper sense a family . . . For those who have no natural family the doors of the great family which is the Church—the Church which finds concrete expression in the diocesan and parish family, in ecclesial basic communities, and in movements of the apostolate—must be opened even wider. No one is without a home and family in this world: the Church is a home and family for everyone, especially those who "labor and are heavy laden" (FC 85).

Teaches the story and traditions of faith

Effective catechesis, both informal and systematic, is an indispensable element of the evangelization done by a community of believers. While Christians believe Jesus was a preacher and healer, Christians also believe that he was a catechist, the fullness of revelation, in every way. Catechesis today must focus on Christ crucified and raised to new life, and on all the traditions, stories, and spiritual practices which have been handed on, as a result, by his followers. *Catechesi Tradendae* put this in perspective:

> The specific character of catechesis, as distinct from the initial . . . proclamation of the Gospel, has the twofold objec-

tive of maturing the initial faith and of educating the true disciple of Christ by means of a deeper and more systematic knowledge of the person and message of our Lord Jesus Christ (CT 19).

Adolescent catechesis should lead young people, "during a delicate period of life," to examine Gospel values and the church's traditions closely. An evangelizing catechesis should be:

capable of leading the adolescent to reexamine his or her life and to engage in dialogue, a catechesis that does not ignore the adolescent's great questions—self giving, belief, love and the means of expressing it constituted by sexuality—such a catechesis can be decisive. The revelation of Jesus Christ as a Friend, Guide, and Model, capable of being admired but also imitated . . . Above all the mysteries of the passion and death of Jesus can speak eloquently to the adolescent's conscience and heart and cast light on (their) first sufferings and on the suffering of the world that (they) are discovering (CT 38).

It is proper, therefore, to say that catechists are, in fact, evangelizers and fulfill tasks which carry great import in the animation of local faith communities (CL 34). With recent powerful shifts in culture and society, particularly in cultural institutions like the family and school systems, we have a radical need for creative models of adolescent catechesis. To that end, the faith community should give catechesis of adolescents and families its best resources in terms of people, energy, organization, and training.

Celebrates the faith story

Vital prayer, preaching, and ritual help the members of the Christian community recall the story of Jesus and celebrate the coming of the reign of God. The church has forcefully called youth ministers recently to discover prayerful ways to share the Word of God which lead young people to interior change (conversion), a growing thirst for Christian community, and a desire for sacramental experiences—especially baptism, reconciliation, and the eucharist. In *News That Is Good*, Bob Hater takes it one step further.

In the ministry of worship an individual or community celebrates the living Lord as central to life. Church liturgy provides opportunities to celebrate human joys and struggles as people link their experiences with Jesus' story (Hater 105).

Prayer services, liturgy of the Word, and heartfelt preaching (homilies) are quite important to celebrating the faith story with assemblies of young people today. Effective use of storytelling, image, symbol, and various kinds of media, during prayer and ritual experiences with adolescents, can increase the evangelizing impact of such moments.

Is inclusive

The sin of discrimination leads to the exclusion of persons on the basis of race, sex, family makeup, age, economic status, or religious beliefs. It is the antithesis of Christian welcome, friendship, and hospitality. Christian solidarity—the acceptance of and communion with the interests and needs of another—should be an aim for which the Christian evangelizer strives every time he or she sets out to touch the life of a young person.

Christ's disciples are challenged to live as an "organic communion." A community which is "catholic" must, necessarily, be characterized by much racial, cultural and economic diversity. Christian faith trusts that the Spirit makes it possible for each and every person to make a unique contribution to the Christian body on earth. Evangelizers who reach out to youth must honor the various religious and cultural traditions of the local communities and households in which young people live. Rather than exclude those who might seem different, youth evangelization efforts, whatever their pastoral forms or settings, should try to incorporate the symbols, stories, rituals, and other gifts which ethnic traditions have to offer to the Church as a whole.

Invites responsible participation by young people

Adolescents can be called to a discipleship exercised through ministry within their faith communities or through service to the wider society. As evangelizing entities, parishes and schools have an obligation to proclaim the Good News and a responsibility to involve others in the Christian mission. Baptized youth are co-responsible for this universal mission. It has long been recognized that Catholic youth ministry should work to help adolescents and adults realize this. Three widely-acknowledged youth ministry goals say:

- Youth ministry works to foster the total personal and spiritual growth of each young person. (This goal emphasizes the personal, "becoming" dimension of human life.)
- Youth ministry seeks to draw young people into responsible participation in the life, mission, and work of the faith community. (This goal emphasizes belonging and communal engagement as dimensions of Christian existence.)
- Youth ministry strives to empower young people to transform the world as disciples of Jesus Christ. (This goal emphasizes the social/ public dimension of human life.) (Roberto 86–87).

A mark of effective evangelization is that it will involve adolescents in ministry. Often, churches neglect the gifts young people have to offer and fail to see young people as necessary to the Christian mission. Some adolescents are ready and willing to take their places, as hard workers, in the ministries of the church community, but they need training and genuine support to do so (*Vision* 20). Other young people long to be of service in the wider community, often directing their attention to justice issues, environmental concerns, or other youth who need someone who will listen and understand. Evangelizing communities find ways for them to do so.

Involves adults in the mission

There is a special need today for adults who will share faith with adolescents, in the name of the Christian community, in a spiritually healthy manner. What are some characteristics of believers such as this? They are adults who are living witnesses to Christian faith, who have experienced lifelong Christian conversion, who authentically believe in the significance of trusting relationships with youth, and who are willing and able to share their faith stories with adolescents without hesitation.

Paul VI spoke compellingly about what youth seek from adult witnesses. They seek authenticity and Christian commitment. They "have a horror of the artificial or false and . . . they are searching above all for truth and honesty." Young people want signs from adult witnesses that will give them answers to questions.

> We are being asked: Do you really believe what you are pro-claiming? Do you live what you believe? Do you really preach what you live? (EN 76).

I am reminded of an often-quoted passage of *Evangelii Nuntiandi* by these questions. That document noted that modern men and women listen more willingly to witnesses than to teachers, and if they listen to teachers at all it is because they are witnesses (EN 41).

Lay persons have a unique role in handing on the Gospel on behalf of the Christian community. They assume responsibilities in the civic community. Many experience first-hand the ups and downs of contemporary household life. Many face, daily, the harsh problems and stresses which modern life serves up. Yet somehow they have found a way to have faith. Somehow they have overcome in themselves, and search for ways to help overcome in others, the separation of the Good News from daily life. In taking up challenges like work and family, they can bring to their ministry with youth a lifestyle that is genuinely inspired and strengthened by the Gospel.

COLLABORATIVE PARTNERSHIPS IN THE MISSION OF YOUTH EVANGELIZATION

The purpose of this chapter has been to investigate the co-discipleship of all baptized members in the evangelizing community of Christ. Christians (or the various Christian churches) have sometimes been called a community of disciples, a term recently popularized by the work of theologian Avery Dulles. The Church's timeless mandate to evangelize derives from the call to holiness which the Lord personally hands on to all persons in his community of disciples. Christian holiness refers to a lifestyle which focuses on special dedication to the Creator's will and to fulfillment of the reign of God. Just as Jesus of Nazareth was holy in this sense, so Church members are called to be holy. In a very broad sense, whenever a member of the Christian community uses his or her God-given charisms, to realize the reign of God here-and-now, we can say that person has acted as an evangelizing minister.

Bob Hater tells an engaging little story in *News That Is Good* that speaks to this fact (Hater 12–13).

> Jim and Sally live in a small Midwestern town. Now retired, they enjoy walking through shops, greeting old friends and meeting new ones. One afternoon they saw a young woman walking alone. She was a newcomer. They welcomed her. The woman's name was Connie.
>
> Soon Connie, Jim and Sally sat in an ice cream parlor. Connie was sad, so Jim and Sally invited her to their home. After a nice dinner and personal conversation, Connie expressed tremendous gratitude, then told them she must leave town. Bill and Sally never saw her again.
>
> On Holy Thursday, five years later, they received a package. Opening it up, Sally found a small frayed teddy bear and a letter which read:
>
>> Dear Sally and Jim,
>>
>> It's been a long time since we met. Remember five years ago when you bought me ice cream, invited me to your home for dinner and listened to me? I was depressed but never told you why. The evening before, I learned I was pregnant. Unmarried and 19, I panicked, ran away, got off the bus in your town and thought of killing myself. When I left, Jim said, "Trust God, and you will be okay." These words, your kindness and God's help saved my life. Enclosed find a small teddy bear. It is frayed and worn. This was my baby Erica's first toy. I want you to have it, as a reminder that two people, myself and little Erica, owe you our lives. Thank you for giving us life. We are now fine. I pray that I can do for others what you have done for us.
>>
>> Love,
>> Connie

Do you think Sally and Jim were taking part in the Christian evangelizing mission? Were they, without show or pretense, trying to be holy? If you say yes you understand key terms in light of contemporary Catholic understandings.

Of course, the natural temptation today among many like Jim and Sally—and among many of the Christian community's leaders and ministry staffs as well—is to lose sight of the Connies of this world. David Bohr reminds us:

> it is so easy . . . to slip into a maintenance mentality. Our churches can easily provide the comfortable pew where we simply bask in the consoling news of God's love and plead that he lend an attentive ear to our self-interest and private concerns. Ministry within the churches then becomes a matter of pastoral maintenance and customer satisfaction. Parishes become country clubs of the saved. (Members) simply expect the Church to supply the needed religious and social services (Bohr 41–42).

Charles Shelton, in his book *Adolescent Spirituality*, has called this maintenance syndrome—when practiced by Catholics in youth ministry—a "reverse evangelization." So what do Christian communities—with pastoral ministry coordinators taking the lead—do to overcome this tendency toward inertia? We find ways to motivate the many Jim's and Sally's in our church to actively live gospel values in all their encounters. We nurture a sense of partnership and Christian adventure in all individuals and groups in our Christian koinonia; they all have a share in the mission. Among ministry team members, we strive for a convergence model of evangelization, to use a favored term of Patrick Brennan. A convergence model (also called an alliance model) is constructed when all people, especially leaders, in a local community's ministry—representing all kinds of pastoral work—share their visions, talents, and resources collaboratively (as co-disciples) to better undertake their common Christian obligation to evangelize the contemporary world (Brennan 1987).

The Challenge of Catholic Youth Evangelization hints at something mentioned early in this chapter. The Spirit of Christ is the source of power and life animating all the agents of Christian evangelization. The Spirit helps people read the signs of the times and become energized and allied for their evangelizing tasks (EN 75; *Challenge* 23). Certain people within the overall evangelizing community have special impacts on adolescents and special roles in sharing faith with them. And something special is occurring among them. In many local communities, these people are talking now about how to realize a dream rooted in the Gospel. They are talking about what it will take to get all people in the church to cooperate and form alliances, pastorally, in the Spirit, in order to read the signs of the times and better share Christian faith with the young. And just who are these special agents of evangelization, the ones beginning to dialogue about how to pastorally collaborate on behalf of adolescents?

Family Members

The family is the basic cell and cradle of evangelization, since God is first revealed to human beings in and through family life. Christian tradition holds that the family household is an *ecclesia domestica*—a Church in miniature and a Church of the home. As John Paul II has indicated, "To the extent (to) which the Christian family accepts the Gospel and matures in faith, it becomes an evangelizing community" (FC 52).

Thus, it is simply wrong to image the family as an object "out there" to be evangelized by church members. Family members evangelize through their Christian witness, the love and forgiveness they share, and the spiritual traditions they cultivate together. Christian households evangelize by sharing faith within the family community and by radiating that faith in the wider society.

The U.S. Catholic bishops have identified four distinctive evangelizing tasks for modern families:

- form an intimate, Christian community;
- hand on moral values and spiritual traditions to family members, while developing the potential of each person;
- participate in the development of society by preparing members to become involved, responsibly, as Christians in the world; and
- become a believing community which is in dialogue with the Creator and at the service of humanity (FC 21).

The Christian family's special vocation is to witness to the Lord's abiding care and love. Today, parents and others are quite often challenged to support and understand members of their family who have become disillusioned, even alienated, when it comes to the church. Such demanding situations call Christian families to live their special vocation most radically. But of course there are many other ways the family can be encouraged to give daily witness to the Lord's concern for humanity. Some of these evangelizing methods have been identified by John Roberto in *Families And Youth: A Resource Manual*:

1) celebrating the faith through rituals, 2) telling the Catholic faith story, 3) enriching family relationships, 4) praying together as a family, 5) performing acts of justice and service, and 6) sharing as a family in wider-community groups or activities (Roberto 118).

Parish Community Members At-Large

All aspects of parish existence "have potential for evangelizing young people who are seeking a deeper spiritual life within the community and those who have not yet . . . heard the call of Christ" (*Challenge* 24). Concerned members of the church parish-at-large recognize this and work hard to discover ways the parish will communicate a message of hope and hospitality to the young.

A parish evangelizes best, as a whole body, when Christian people gather on a regular basis "to profess belief in Jesus, engage in ritual worship, and serve the kingdom," (Hater 59) thus illuminating for all to see the God who is already present in our families and our neighborhoods.

In recent days, many parishioners in the average Catholic community have acknowledged the importance of youth to the Christian body. Sometimes this has only been lip service. Sometimes it has been well intentioned, but lacking in true support or generous resourcing for youth ministry. Challenges which consciousness-raised Catholic parish members are now talking about—in relation to youth and family evangelization—include:

- how the parish can give attention to those geographical areas and cultural settings—in which youth can be found—which remain largely uninfluenced by the Gospel message;
- how to help young people and others link their everyday lives and activities with challenges presented by Gospel values;
- how to stop clinging, in co-dependent ways, to outmoded structures, practices, and symbols that no longer work for the parish's cause of Christian evangelization (Crosby 1991); and
- how to welcome and include—not "screen out" or avoid the inactive Christians, the alienated, the challenged, and the strangers who could draw spirit and hope from a vital Church community (Brennan 195).

On those last points, Pat Brennan's, *Parishes That Excel*, presents a pastoral (strategic) agenda—with many practical steps and parish success stories—for those communities which strive to fully embrace anew their central mission of evangelization (Brennan 14–20). As usual, his work demonstrates the role of the entire parish in an alliance ministry approach to total Christian evangelization.

Representatives of Catholic Schools

Catholic schools are challenged to integrate evangelizing experiences into all aspects of school community life. Regretfully, many young people today experience their high school as their primary faith community, because average local parishes have little or nothing meaningful to offer them. Thus, all those who participate in Catholic school life—students, faculty, administration, and other staff—share immediately in the responsibility to make their campuses into communities which live and breathe the Gospel.

Through the school, "the local church evangelizes, educates, and contributes to the formation of a healthy and morally sound lifestyle among its members." In its work to educate the young, the Catholic school strives to convey "a sense of the nature of Christianity, and of how Christians are trying to live their lives" (RD 69).

The challenge to evangelize young people through Catholic school communities seems more urgent in our day, in some respects, than in the past. Developing community and living together as a faith community have become primary, explicit goals for every Catholic school since many natural communities today (e.g., families, neighborhoods, parishes, and racial and ethnic groups) have been diminished by powerful cultural forces. The unique identity of the Catholic school, however, is found not in community but precisely in the religious formation which is integrated into the total education which the school offers adolescents. Christian religious educators and campus youth ministries work hard to teach young people to be open to God's Word, to build community, and to live lives which incorporate regular times of prayer, ritual, and caring service for others.

The Catholic school, naturally, then should seek a partnership with local church parishes, and local parishes should seek partnerships with representatives of the local Catholic school(s). Given the components of

Catholic education—ministries of Word, worship, community-building, and Christian service—and given their staffs of Christian witnesses present to young people for many hours every school day, representatives of the Catholic school have much to add to any dialogue about how to evangelize adolescents. In the best of circumstances, they should likewise be open enough to hear those suggestions which representatives of church parishes and other faith communities have about how to enrich the faith-formation which the Catholic school provides.

Young People

To the church community, adolescents and children often symbolize both exceptional potential and a challenge misunderstood. Young people are not the church's burden. They are the Christian community's hope!

By their baptism, Christian youth are called to the mission of evangelization. It would be wrong to continue to see them merely as objects of pastoral concern. It is sinful to just talk about them critically or talk down to them as if the Spirit of Christ cannot animate them as it animates others in the faith community.

Many young people long to be given a voice in their church. They often want to serve the faith community at large, share faith with their peers, or reach out to the surrounding culture in Christian service. They want to engage in things which give meaning to their lives. They hunger for recognition in their parish or school family, especially from those adults whom they respect and trust.

As we have mentioned before, an authentic understanding of youth ministry recognizes that youth are very much capable of vital, co-responsible Gospel proclamation and discipleship. However, as the new *Challenge* paper notes:

> this call to discipleship—to taking on the values, actions, and qualities of Jesus—is conditioned by young people's personal and faith development and their situations in life. The principle of "developmental discipleship" requires that the call to mission and the response of young people be age-appropriate and that our expectations be realistic (*Challenge* 13).

In the years to come, young people will continue to take on importance in the overall effort to evangelize the world. They have much to say and much to offer today. For example, anyone who has ever been present at a youth retreat or youth assembly, at which an effective peer minister personally spoke up in testimony to the love of the Lord, knows firsthand that adolescents usually listen willingly to adolescent witnesses because they speak the same language. Yes, young people have much to say—to other youth and to the adult faith community as well—and many are hoping for meaningful ways to say their word. As Paul VI urged, young people trained in faith and prayer must become, more and more, apostles to the human community. The church must learn to make more possible their contribution (EN 72).

Leaders in Pastoral Ministry

All leaders in the faith community share in the responsibility to evangelize young people. Evangelization is the heart and lifeblood of all intentional ministries. Those in direct ministries to adolescents have a special responsibility in the mission, though, since they create the outreach strategies and faith-development programs that foster youth evangelization (*Challenge* 24).

The ongoing duty which ministry leaders accept has both explicit and implicit dimensions. Ministry leaders must collaborate to find ways by which young people can explicitly and verbally hear proclamations of the Gospel, through the varied ministries a local community sponsors and without which "there is no true evangelization" (EN 22). They must also seek to communicate the Good News non-verbally, or implicitly, through their lifestyles and witness to God's love for all human beings. All ministers are challenged to "be the story," in the flesh, for adolescents (*Challenge* 11).

A particular gift which parish and school ministry leaders can give to the mission of evangelization is a humble willingness to collaborate with others in faith. From the fertile turf of Christian collaboration, new and prophetic alliances, organizations, church structures, and ministries can spring up. Holistic (or convergent) pastoral models which will serve adolescents and their families, which venture beyond the walls of the church and parish grounds are things we particularly need to evolve in the '90s. Of course, collaboration and communication will only take root, among members of ministry leadership teams, if those team members first look to their own houses and develop a renewed desire for that Christian holiness which characterizes people on an evangelizing journey and those who dare keep hope in the Lord alive.

BACK TO THE FUTURE

What can we know about the future shapes of evangelization in the overall evangelizing community? Building on the signs of the times, William Rademacher says:

> Some of today's trends in the development of ministry can be expected to continue. We can anticipate new ministries in the areas of preaching, theology, teaching, physical and psychological healing, social reconciliation, peace-making, family life, communications, counseling, government, international development, the arts, and domestic celebration.
>
> Surely there will be an increase of ministries by and to minorities. Ministry will become more professional and will include more women. Ministers will continue to serve in marriage encounter, cursillo, and the charismatic renewal. There will be an increasing diversity and more adaptability in the churches. The present declericalization of the ministry is bound to continue. Ministers will be more mobile because of the increasing mobility of society itself. More and more ministers will have a part-time ministry, e.g., teaching a religious education class in the evening after working at the post office during the day. The rate of vocational change will continue to be high. Greater responsibilities and positions of leadership will be entrusted to ministers at earlier ages.
>
> In the future we will see a greater use of commitment to ministry for limited terms, i.e., three, six, ten years (Rademacher 226–227).

Regarding the future shapes of evangelizing youth ministries, let's go back for a moment to St. Nobody's and St. Gospela's communities. What should they do to better reveal the face of God to the young men and women they could reach? In fact, what could your local faith community—or mine for that matter—do today to prepare for a more Christian tomorrow?

The Challenge of Catholic Youth Evangelization dramatically calls members of the Christian community, as a whole, to first examine their current approaches to youth evangelization. In fact, drawing on the prophetic call issued by the Catholic Bishops of the United States in their recent statement *Go and Make Disciples* (1993), the *Challenge* indicates that such a self-examination is the "first task for those responsible for the faith community's ministry to young people in all settings: parish, school, diocese, and other youth-serving organizations and programs" (*Challenge* 25).

A Christian community's honest, critical reflection on its current efforts to evangelize adolescents will lead it to the following challenging questions:

- What must we do now to more effectively reach out to unchurched and un-Gospeled young people in our surroundings?
- What steps must we take to shape a more inclusive, welcoming, and hospitable Christian body?
- What steps must we take to improve the quality of worship experiences for our people and to involve young people more meaningfully in our community's rituals?
- How can we integrate a family perspective into all of our evangelizing activities?
- What should we change in order to improve the ways we, as a staff, proclaim the Gospel implicitly and explicitly to others, especially the young?
- What special forms of support can we provide to adolescents on their journey toward Christian conversion?
- What steps should we engage in to improve the quality of and the models of adolescent catechesis provided by our faith community?
- In what ways will we renew our efforts to challenge young people to respond to the call of Christian discipleship?
- What further planning and inspiration do we require in order to integrate an evangelizing element into all aspects of our community's ministry to adolescents and their families? (*Challenge* 25).

A critical hour has indeed come for those communities that want to share faith in the name of Jesus, the original Evangelizer. A new missionary age is upon us, like it or not, and it is our particular challenge to find the means that will create a deep hunger and thirst for the gospel in those who have marginally heard it and in those contemporary millions who have not yet encountered it at all. New frontiers stretch out into neighborhoods, shopping malls, city streets, and households all around us. These new frontiers constitute the turfs on which the mission, which has a church and an evangelizing people, will finally be fulfilled.

Works Cited

Bohr, David. "Becoming and Sharing the Good News: The Nature and Content of Evangelization." *Catholic Evangelization Today.* Ed. Kenneth Boyack C.S.P. New York: Paulist Press, 1987.

Brennan, Patrick J. "Catholic Evangelization in the United States: An Agenda for the Future," *Catholic Evangelization Today.* Ed. Kenneth Boyack C.S.P. New York: Paulist Press, 1987.

Brennan, Patrick J. *The Evangelizing Parish.* Allen TX: Tabor Publishing, 1987.

Brennan, Patrick J. *Parishes That Excel.* New York: Crossroad Publishing Co., 1992.

Congregation for Catholic Education. *The Religious Dimension of Education in a Catholic School: Guidelines for Reflection and Renewal.* Rome, 1988.

Crosby, Michael. *The Dysfunctional Church.* Notre Dame: Ave Marie Press, 1991.

Gallup, George. *Forecast 2000.* New York: William Morrow and Co., 1984.

Haring, Bernard. *Evangelization Today.* New York: Crossroad Publishing Co., 1991.

Hater, Robert J. *News That Is Good.* Notre Dame: Ave Marie Press, 1990.

John Paul II. *Catechesi Tradendae.* Washington, DC: USCC Publishing, 1979.

John Paul II. *Christifideles Laici.* Washington, DC: USCC Publishing, 1988.

John Paul II. *Familiaris Consortio.* Washington, DC: USCC Publishing, 1981.

John Paul II. *Redemptoris Missio.* Washington, DC: USCC Publishing, 1990.

McBrien, Richard. *Catholicism.* Minneapolis: Winston Press, 1980.

National Federation for Catholic Youth Ministry. *The Challenge of Catholic Youth Evangelization: Called to be Witnesses and Storytellers.* New Rochelle NY: Don Bosco Multimedia, 1993.

Paul VI. *Evangelii Nuntiandi.* Washington, DC: USCC Publishing, 1975.

Rademacher, William J. *Lay Ministry: A Theological, Spiritual, and Pastoral Handbook.* New York: Crossroad Publishing Co., 1992.

Roberto, John. "Affirmations for Faith Growth and Faith Sharing in Families." *Families and Youth: A Resource Manual.* Ed. Leif Kehrwald and John Roberto. New Rochelle NY: Don Bosco Multimedia, 1992).

Roberto, John, editor. *Access Guides to Youth Ministry: Early Adolescent Ministry.* New Rochelle NY: Don Bosco Multimedia, 1991.

United States Catholic Conference. *A Vision of Youth Ministry.* Washington DC:
USCC, 1986.

DOCUMENTS CITED:

CL *Christifideles Laici* (The Lay Members of Christ's Faithful People)
CT *Catechesi Tradendae* (On Catechesis in Our Time)
EN *Evangelii Nuntiandi* (On Evangelization in the Modern World)
FC *Familiaris Consortio* (Role of the Christian Family in the Modern
      World)
RD *The Religious Dimension of Education in a Catholic School*
RM *Redemptoris Missio* (Mission of the Redeemer)

CHAPTER 9

EMPOWERING ADULT LEADERS FOR EVANGELIZATION

REYNOLDS R. EKSTROM

The faith community must call forth caring, committed adults who want to minister to, with and for young people. Integral to this ministry are adults who like young people, who are spiritually healthy and rooted in prayer, who live their faith, and who are open to ongoing, personal conversion. Adults who are able to share their faith story and who are willing to enter into relationships of mutual trust, acceptance and respect are vital if the community is to effectively minister to young people.

—The Challenge of Catholic Youth Evangelization

THE WORD *EMPOWER* MEANS TO COMMISSION, delegate, or give some kind of authorization to another. From the earliest days following the initial publication of *A Vision of Youth Ministry*, it has been widely recognized that the empowerment of adult Christians to reach out to and share faith with adolescents—in the name of the entire Christian community—is an essential element of a ministry which will be, in fact, "good news" for young people.

A Vision of Youth Ministry noted:

> Adults, faith-filled Christians, are the very center of ministry
> with youth—adults who are in touch with their faith, living the
> Gospel in all aspects of their lives. Young people look for mod-
> els, persons they can look up to, and not simply persons with
> whom they can build a peer relationship. Some qualities that
> should characterize an adult involved in youth ministry are: the
> quality of presence that a person brings to time spent with the
> young, the ability to listen deeply to others, the ability to be
> comfortable in a variety of different settings, and the ability to
> speak credibly of one's own faith experiences (*Vision* 20–21).

Adults who will spend time with young people, build relationships
with them, and share the Gospel—through living witness, engaging words,
and self-giving deeds—in ways that prove meaningful to young people
remain, today, at the center of the Church's mission to evangelize adolescents. A piece of wisdom shared first by Michael Warren in the early
'70s and then again, in 1976, in *A Vision of Youth Ministry*, has become
even more true as the years have gone by. "What the young need today
are not adults who will (simply) hand over information, but adults who
will hand over themselves and the secret of their own faith" (Warren 29–
39; *Vision* 21). Of course, Paul VI had said as much, in a very engaging
way, a year earlier in his exhortation *On Evangelization in the Modern
World*: modern youth listen more willingly to witnesses than to teachers.
If they listen to teachers at all, it is because they are living, Christian
witnesses (EN 41).

EMPOWERMENT FOR MINISTRY: ROOTED IN THE SPIRIT

The tradition of the church is that all baptized persons have a role in the
church community's essential witness and mission, called evangelization.

In that regard, Paul VI taught clearly that the Spirit is the "principal agent
of evangelization." The Holy Spirit first impels individuals to share the good
news of Jesus with others through life witness and inspiring words. And the
Spirit causes human beings, ultimately, to become inclined to hear, compre-
hend, and accept the one, true gospel in good conscience (EN 75).

The gift of the Spirit, received in Christian baptism, authorizes and in a way delegates and empowers each of us to do the work of Christian witness, outreach, and proclamation. In the context of an evangelizing youth ministry, as noted in *The Challenge of Catholic Youth Evangelization*, it can be said:

> Evangelization will never be possible without the action of the Holy Spirit. The Spirit is the source of power and life behind all of the other agents (in Christian ministry) . . . Through the Holy Spirit the Gospel penetrates to the heart of the world, for it is the Spirit who causes people to discern the "signs of the times," which evangelization reveals and puts to use with history. It is the Spirit who energizes the community for the task of evangelization (*Challenge* 23).

The Catholic bishops of the United States have spoken compellingly, with images rich and attractive, to help us reflect on these matters of Christian faith. In their document *Go and Make Disciples*, they have pointed out:

> The Holy Spirit is the fire of Jesus. The Spirit, the first gift of the risen Christ to his people, gives us both the ability to receive the Gospel of Jesus and, in response, the power to proclaim it. Without the Holy Spirit, evangelization simply cannot occur. The Spirit brings about evangelization in the life of the Church and in the Church's sharing the Gospel with others (*Go and Make Disciples* 5).

In another passage from *Go and Make Disciples*, the bishops say "Jesus set the world on fire, and that blaze goes on even today." The fire of the Lord is communicated to human beings by the Spirit and, thus, the story of Jesus Christ's mission is continued in our lives—our lives today "are part of the story of salvation" (*Go and Make Disciples* 1).

SERIOUS PREPARATION AND TRAINING IS NEEDED

The exhortation to the entire Church is to share the message and values of the gospel of Jesus, using the inspiration, guidance, and hope provided by his Spirit. The "good news" of Christian life is meant for all ears and all hearts, throughout the world, for all time.

> Go, therefore, and make disciples of all nations, baptizing them in the name of the Father, and of the Son, and of the Holy Spirit, teaching them to observe all that I have commanded you. And behold, I am with you always, until the end of the age (Matthew 28:19–20).

Lay persons, in particular, are urged by the church to evangelize the world—too "evangelize culture," in typical evangelization language—in a special way. Why? Because the lives of contemporary lay persons touch all aspects of human existence and human spiritual longing today. Therefore, lay persons must be empowered to "evangelize culture" by:

> upsetting, as it were, through the power of the Gospel, humankind's criteria of judgment, determining values, points of interest, lines of thought, sources of inspiration and models of life, which are in contrast to the Word of God and (God's) plan of salvation (EN 19).

To many pastoral ministry leaders, the question which occurs is "How can individuals be prepared and enabled for this crucial mission to evangelize culture?" As Marsha Whelan pointed out rather succinctly some years ago, Paul VI, in his document *On Evangelization in the Modern World*, did not give specific guidelines regarding training for Christian evangelizers. He merely said "serious preparation is needed" (EN 73; Whelan 92).

Ms. Whelan, in an essay published in 1987 called "The Workers for Evangelization," addressed the need to train adults to evangelize others. She indicated that training should focus on helping people witness to Christian hope and concern, in their daily lives, and on helping individuals learn to how to actually proclaim (verbally share) the gospel with others—something which Catholics, generally speaking, "do no know how to do . . ." (Whelan 93).

The essay indicated that the most basic rudiments of any training geared to help adults evangelize culture will include:

- Helping them identify and reflect on the experience of God in their lives, particularly in moments of Christian change and conversion
- Helping adult Catholics articulate, simply and clearly, how God has

called them, at different times, to change and grow

- Equipping adults with methods by which they can share their life stories with others in meaningful ways
- Showing adult Catholics how to share the basic message and values found the gospel and in Catholic tradition
- Helping adults recognize that "the circles in which they travel" are the places in which the Lord wants them to share the gospel with others (Whelan 93).

The document *A Vision of Youth Ministry* was a bit more explicit with regard to the enablement and commissioning of adults who wish to minister to adolescents in the name of Jesus. The *Vision* noted that training and preparation for evangelizing youth—a "practical" ministry training which, ideally, ought to be both initial and ongoing—should focus on

- Helping the prospective minister to further his or her spiritual growth
- Encouraging them to "review their own spiritual lives" and gifts for ministry, given by the Spirit
- Increasing the minister's knowledge of Scripture and Christian doctrine
- Increasing the minister's knowledge and appreciation for the Catholic vision of youth ministry
- Enabling youth's ministers to use appropriate communication skills and, also, ministry collaboration techniques
- Teaching prospective ministers to adolescents about young people's families, their patterns of faith-development, and the impact of mainstream U.S. pop culture on youth today (*Vision* 21).

A well-conceived and adequately supported program to empower pastoral ministers who reach out to contemporary youth "can launch a strong youth ministry effort" in the local faith community and, in turn, can potentially vitalize all levels of Christian life within the parish, school, and even the diocese in which the preparation-program is situation (*Vision* 21).

What is the ultimate goal of "serious preparation and training" of adults for the Christian evangelization of adolescents? An important clue is included in the text of *The Challenge of Catholic Youth Evangelization*. It says that the preparation and training must exist to call forth and empower:

caring, committed adults who want to minister to, with, and for young people . . . who are spiritually healthy and rooted in prayer, and who are open to ongoing, personal conversion. Adults who are able to share their faith story and who are willing to enter into relationships of mutual trust, acceptance, and respect are vital if the community is to minister effectively to young people (*Challenge* 23).

ESSENTIAL QUALITIES AND COMPETENCIES OF MINISTERS TO YOUTH

The foundational ministry of youth evangelization requires a variety of leaders (e.g., pastor, pastoral associates, DRE, school principal, youth ministry coordinator) and ministry staff members (e.g., parish catechists, retreat team members, youth group staff) collaborating together on behalf of the young. Of course, parents, family members, and the local faith community as a whole make crucial contributions in the church's mission to share the gospel with adolescents. However, parish and school leaders, and members of their pastoral staffs, support and extend, in significant ways, the parts played by families and local church in the faith-development of youth.

It is possible to describe the essential personal qualities and professional-pastoral competencies (knowledge and skills) toward which those who minister to young people should strive. In fact, within a Catholic youth ministry perspective, these personal qualities and pastoral competencies are things which adults should work toward developing on an ongoing basis. In selecting and training adults who wish to work with adolescents in the name of the faith community, pastoral leaders should look for the following personal traits in ministry candidates and look for signs that they are willing to develop the competencies—the essential knowledge base and pastoral skills—which will also be identified.

Personal Traits and Qualities

A person who lives and witnesses to the counter-cultural Gospel of Jesus is one who is personally rooted in the dynamic process of Christian conversion and is personally seeking Christian holiness. In living and choosing ongoing, Christian conversion, on a daily basis, one shows that he or she is becoming more and more devoted to the "good news" of God's offer of salvation. A person, therefore, centers his or her personal life on Christian charity toward all, service to others, and prayerful communion with the Creator. The result is growth in Christian holiness. Holiness, in this respect, refers to a style of life—a fundamental Christian *vocation*—by which one shows that he or she is dedicated to God's revelation in a very special way. Persons who are "holy," yet nevertheless real human beings, fully engaged in the comings and goings of daily life, become more and more committed to moral goodness and to bettering creation for all persons. All Christian conversion and all Christian holiness are inspired by the living witness of Jesus of Nazareth and the immeasurable gift he has given to humanity, the Holy Spirit.

It goes without saying that Christian witnesses who are deeply engaged in ongoing, Christian change and perfection are much needed in ministry with young people today. John Paul II has said, "It is ever more urgent that today all Christians take up again the way of gospel renewal" (CL 16). True witnesses to the gospel should imitate, in every way possible, the example of Jesus. They do so, generally speaking, by listening to the stirrings of the Spirit in their own hearts and, according to John Paul II, by choosing to live in ways appropriate to the follower of the Lord.

> Life according to the Spirit, whose fruit is holiness, stirs up every baptized person and requires each to follow and imitate Jesus Christ in embracing the Beatitudes; in listening and meditating on the Word of God; in conscious and active participation in the liturgical and sacramental life of the Church; in personal prayer; in family or in community; in the hunger for justice; in the practice of commandment of love in all circumstances of life and service (to all), especially the least, the poor and the suffering (CL 16).

A number of concrete, personal qualities and traits appropriate to the evangelizing youth minister can be extrapolated from these insights. In fact, let us name seven qualities of the minister who seeks ongoing, Christian conversion and authentic Christian holiness as a way of life or "vocation." Therefore, things to look for in the person who serves the personal and spiritual needs of adolescents today should be:

■ **Personal faith**—The individual gives witness to a vibrant, personal relationship with God and a well-developed life of prayer. He or she recognizes that a call to exercise gifts from the Spirit has been extended by the Creator.

- **Active witness to the Gospel**—The individual deeply believes in and lives the Christian good news within the Catholic tradition—and he or she wants to share that good news with others. Witness is incorporated into daily life and into explicit ministry activities and relationships.
- **Witness to the Church tradition**—The person in ministry shows that he or she is dedicated to the Catholic community and the mission of the body of Christ.
- **Active participation in the community**—The individual participates, regularly and actively, in the life of the local parish, is willing to extend this participation to friendship and collaboration with other evangelizing ministers, and seems willing to deal with conflict and disagreements in sensitive and understanding ways.
- **Service to the faith community**—The prospective minister indicates, in numerous ways, that he or she is flexible enough to respond, without prodding, to the spiritual needs of individuals, families, wider (civic) community, and neighborhood groups.
- **Love and knowledge of the Gospel**—The individual shows, in many ways, a deep love for the story of Jesus and a desire to share that life-changing story with others. To that end, the person studies and meditates on Scripture regularly and seeks to better understand and properly interpret God's revelation in the Bible.
- **Knowledge of the Catholic faith tradition**—The individual possesses a fundamental understanding of Scripture, doctrine, and the moral teachings of Catholics. He or she indicates a willingness to further personal knowledge about such matters in order to evangelize others more fully.

In all, however, a genuine love for the Lord and a love for young people are perhaps the most critical personal characteristics which any evangelizer must possess. It has long been recognized by many in youth ministry that this Christian love—a true sign of conversion and holiness—will be best expressed by adults who are perceived by young people, and other adults, as *available*, *accepting*, *authentic*, and *vulnerable* (Shelton 16–20).

What does this imply in practical ministry terms? Any encounter with adolescents must be marked by openness on the part of the evangelizer. Openness means presence, *real availability*. Adolescents need and want to know that they are important—welcome to approach an adult to talk, on the adolescent's own terms. Adults who evangelize youth should understand and *accept* the usual questions, struggles, and concerns experienced by young people. They should learn to appreciate young men and women for who they are—persons loved and gifted by God. Adolescents tend to seek out adults who can share their own faith lives—their own struggles, hopes, and doubts—in an *authentic* way. Through such interaction with the young, adults who evangelize demonstrate to youth, quietly but profoundly, an acceptance of the adolescent journey toward personal meaning and faith. Such quiet acceptance, however, also demonstrates a certain *vulnerability*. Adults who can be authentic and real and vulnerable provide tremendous supports to young people. They encourage young people, through Christian humility, to mature in faith and stretch toward adulthood. Whenever a young person perceives an adult Christian witness who is comfortable with himself or herself—especially with his or her personal limitations—but capable of admitting failure and/or the need for further Christian growth in conversion and holiness, the way is opened up for adolescent self-acceptance and deeper acceptance of the Christian good news for the journey.

MINISTRY COMPETENCIES (KNOWLEDGE AND SKILLS)

Those who reach out to young people in faith approach their tasks with varying degrees of knowledge and competence. Therefore, programs of self-directed study and organized training modules, for groups and staffs of ministers, should be designed and implemented to help individuals acquire the ministry knowledge and skills they need. The whole Christian community, through diocesan offices, parishes, schools, universities, regional formation centers, and the like, should be engaged in the formation and training of evangelizing ministers to youth. Training will include spiritual and theological growth of the ministry candidate. And it will include the development of skills and methodologies necessary to share faith, effectively, with adolescents.

Any attempt to build the ministry competencies of adults who work with young people today should be centered on the following areas.

The Spirituality of the Evangelizer

The evangelizing youth minister should demonstrate:

- a willingness and ability to speak with conviction about his or her

life of faith and faith convictions as a member of the Catholic Christian tradition;
- a continuing growth in his or her personal prayer and in communal participation in prayer and ritual;
- an ability to see God's activity in his or her life experience, lifestyle, and ministry.

Knowledge of the Adolescent

The evangelizing youth minister should demonstrate a foundational understanding of:

- the essential characteristics of adolescent growth and development as drawn from the fields of psychology, sociology, family studies, and faith-development—and how these relate directly to the mission to evangelize young people;
- the characteristics, trends, and mainstream cultural values in America; the characteristics of ethnic cultures; and the impact of social trends and values on the lives of youth;
- the signs, symbols, images, language, and "youth culture" of contemporary adolescents and how these relate to a Christian inculturation process directed toward adolescents and their families.

Basic Skills for Youth Evangelization

The adult who wishes to evangelize adolescents should demonstrate basic abilities and skills:

- Ability to do outreach to young people—to befriend them and to build relationships with them;
- Ability to develop and take part in gospel proclamation experiences for youth, using personal storytelling techniques, other group activities and group-based processes, media and various other resources appropriate to such evangelizing experiences;
- Skill in relating the gospel message and values to the world of adolescents—using youth's own language(s), signs, symbols, stories, and images;
- Skill in using communication techniques, group discussion meth-

ods, community-building methods, and "theological reflection" style dialogues;

■ Ability to share faith personally and deeply with others;
■ Skill in challenging young people and others to accept the gospel and to enter more fully into the life of the Christian community;
■ Ability to prepare and conduct various types of prayer experiences, worship services, ritual formats, and service experiences with and for young people.

Content of the Gospel Message

The adult who intends to evangelize young people should demonstrate a fundamental grasp of the following:

■ key themes in the Hebrew Scriptures and Christian Scriptures, and ways to utilize the tools of scripture scholarship and analysis to interpret the Bible;
■ the meaning of the life, mission, death, and resurrection of Jesus Christ to Christian community and all of humanity;
■ the Church's contemporary approach to interpretation and understanding of the Christ-event;
■ the images and models of the Church used today, particularly the notion of Church as "community of disciples," and also basic insight into the Church's mission and ministries in a multicultural, multiracial world environment;
■ contemporary sacramental theology and the role of the sacraments in Christian existence;
■ Catholic Christian moral expressions and teachings—including the concepts of personal sin, social sin, the power of God's revelation and grace, and appropriate moral decision-making skills;
■ major themes in the Church's teachings on social justice and peace, and how these relate to the world of young people today;
■ the core doctrines, religious values, and religious practices of Catholic Christianity today and how these are expressed in the life of the church community today.

Works Cited

John Paul II. *Christifideles Laici* (*Lay Members of Christ's Faithful People*), 1988.

National Conference of Catholic Bishops (NCCB). *Go and Make Disciples: A National Plan and Strategy for Catholic Evangelization in the United States.* Washington, DC: USCC, 1993.

National Federation for Catholic Youth Ministry (NFCYM). *The Challenge of Catholic Youth Evangelization: Called to be Witnesses and Storytellers.* New Rochelle, NY: DBM, 1993.

Paul VI. *Evangelii Nuntiandi.* (*On Evangelization in the Modern World*), 1975.

Shelton, Charles. *Adolescent Spirituality.* New York: Crossroad Publishing, 1983.

A Vision of Youth Ministry. Washington, DC: USCC, 1986 Edition.

Warren, Michael. *A Future for Youth Catechesis.* New York: Paulist Press, 1975.

Whelan, Marsha. "The Workers for Evangelization," *Catholic Evangelization Today: A New Pentecost for the United States.* Ed. Kenneth Boyack, CSP. New York: Paulist Press, 1987.

CHAPTER 10

EMPOWERING ADOLESCENTS FOR EVANGELIZATION: ONE PARISH'S STORY

FRAY GILBERTO CAVAZOS, OFM

Youth, too, are called to be evangelizers. "Young people trained in faith and prayer must become more and more the apostles of youth. The Church counts greatly on their contribution" (EN, no. 72). Through their witness to the importance of faith in their lives, their expression of faith through service to others, and their participation in personal and communal prayer and worship, young people evangelize their peers. This is a most powerful agent for evangelization.

—The Challenge of Catholic Youth Evangelization

INTRODUCTION

My involvement in youth evangelization began six years ago when I was first stationed at Nuestra Senora de los Angeles as Parochial Vicar. When I arrived, the parish had just adopted a parish plan from Mexico City called *El Sistema Integral de Evangelizacion*, the System of Integral Evangelization (SINE). SINE called for division of our parish of 18,000 families into seven geographical sectors and the development of home-based communities for each sector by way of an Evangelization Retreat.

Nuestra Senora de los Angeles is a Franciscan parish on the southwest side of San Antonio, Texas. It is about 98% Hispanic, primarily Mexican and Mexican-American. The parish itself is made up of two groups of people, a somewhat mobile lower class who rent homes in the area for a few years and then move on and a stable lower middle class community. This second group is composed primarily of the old guard who have been around since the founding of the parish and their children, many of which no longer live within the parish boundaries but continue to come to the parish from different parts of the city and the suburbs.

The attraction, I believe, at Nuestra Senora de los Angeles is that it is a very Hispanic community. There is only one English Mass here during the whole week. Every other liturgy is celebrated either in Spanish or is bilingual.

One thing I have noticed about Neustra Senora de los Angeles, over the years, is that people involved in its ministry, primarily, are either the elderly or the youth. Middle-age parishioners are not well represented within the ranks of ministers. I believe this to be true because of the economic situation of families in the parish. All parents definitely need to work in order to pay the bills and provide little extras for their children.

Although the parish is, primarily and economically, a poor parish, we are a parish that is rich in lay ministers and in lay ministry teams, thanks to the works of evangelization. One of these teams is the Tropa de Cristo. La Tropa de Cristo is a Franciscan youth evangelization team which has grown out of my work with and interest in youth ministry and evangelization. La Tropa de Cristo was developed due to a need to adapt SINE's evangelization retreat to the high school level for use in our catechetical program for adolescents. What was supposed to be a one-time retreat team activity has developed into an organized ministry which has traveled through Texas, and to places as far away as Nebraska and Illinois to evangelize both youth and adults.

WHY YOUTH EVANGELIZATION?

In reality, when I look back over my involvement with youth evangelization I cannot honestly say that I chose it. Rather, I would say it chose me. My involvement in youth evangelization was quite accidental. When I arrived in the parish to which I was recently assigned, I was asked to do high school catechesis. Actually, I had no idea of what I would do. At the same time I was asked to help form adults who would help in the SINE evangelization program. And so, due to my involvement with adult evangelization, I began to try different ways of evangelizing youth. This eventually led to La Tropa de Cristo.

I never really set out to form the Tropa de Cristo. The Tropa de Cristo, so it seems, formed naturally, in response to the call of God, in order to evangelize youth within our parish boundaries and wherever it was that we were invited to go. As we have seen the Tropa de Cristo's ministry grow, we have had to evaluate its progress and set up goals. However, the original team goal was quite simple. It was that the members of La Tropa would plan and execute evangelization retreats and workshops well.

There have been two personal youth evangelization goals for which I have seen a need and which I have worked to implement, especially within the last year and a half. The first has been to slowly wean team members away from me and show them that they are quite capable of doing ministry by themselves. It is my feeling that any ministry is meant not to glorify the minister but rather to enable those being ministered to. I thank God that Tropa de Cristo is not dependent upon me. Rather, members have been enabled and enlivened to do God's work without my presence. The other goal has been to inspire the young people in La Tropa to follow Jesus Christ according to the way of San Francisco de Assisi. I do not mean that I want them all to become religious community members. Far from it. Rather, I want them, as lay people, to follow Jesus Christ in the spirit of simplicity, purity, and commitment in the spirit of Francisco.

YOUTH AS EVANGELIZERS

Let us consider Hispanic young persons as evangelizers, serving within the community of the great Evangelist, the Church.

Circumstances invite us to make special mention of the young. Their increasing number and growing presence in society and likewise the problems assailing them should awaken in every one the desire to offer them with zeal and intelligence the Gospel ideal as something to be known and lived. And on the other hand, young people who are well trained in faith and prayer must become more and more the apostles of youth. The Church counts greatly on their contribution, and we ourself have often manifested our full confidence in them (EN 72).

The Latin American Bishops meeting in Puebla, Mexico in 1979 saw that many young people have grown disillusioned by a lack of authentic leaders and disgusted with consumerism. These young people seem to have lost hope. However, there are many other young people who "want to respond to the many different forms of egotism (in our world) by constructing a world of peace and justice and love" (DP 1177). In evangelized youth who have experienced the joy of giving themselves to Jesus the Church finds "an enormous force for renewal" (DP 1178). These young people will question the Church, challenge it, and call it to be rejuvenated. The Church should see in these young people real potential for the future of evangelization because they bring a real dynamism to it. Young people should be invited therefore to be part of the Church's evangelizing activity so as to build up a "civilization of love," showing preference to the poor (DP 1186–1188). Both the documents of Puebla and *Evangelii Nuntiandi* show the Church's confidence in youth today and express hope that Christian youth will be able to evangelize other youth and bring them into the community of believers.

Youth is an age of transition. Young people are persons in a process of growth. They look for their own identities and for definition as members of society. Even though youth journey through a transitional stage of life we need to help them realize that this stage is, in and of itself, important. When they are not taken seriously, youth move away from the adult community in a variety of directions. "What disorients young people most is the threat to their need for authenticity by the adult environment which is largely inconsistent and manipulative; by the generation gap; by a consumer civilization; by a certain instinct-oriented pedagogy; and by drugs, sexualism, and the temptation to atheism" (DP 1171).

Good youth ministry programs take the young person seriously, as a whole being, not just as someone going through a phase. Hispanic young people, in general, need a lot of affirmation and acceptance. They usually rely heavily on peers for these. During adolescence, the need for peer support and acceptance is especially important. As Tom Zanzig has said, the uneasiness and occasional pain associated with all the changes in puberty often lead young people to look to peers for support and security . . . but it is also during this time that adolescents need to begin moving away from their near total dependence upon their parents.

This time of transition for Hispanic youth is particularly challenging in the United States. The adolescent transition, for them, involves moving from total dependence upon their parents but also toward an even greater independence, i.e., toward the integration of two cultures in one person. In this greater movement, Hispanic youth become bi-cultural, bi-lingual, and bi-cognitive.

According to the III Encuentro Nacional, Hispanic youth today are hungry for formation. They need Church to provide them with programs that are sensitive to their reality; programs that help foster a bi-cultural identity; programs that celebrate Hispanic religiosity; programs that foster youth leadership; programs that reach out to the alienated; and, finally, programs which train Hispanic youth to be leaders.

Hispanic young people today are greatly influenced by their environment. The Latin American Bishops dedicated a chapter of the Puebla documents to "A Preferential Option for Young People." In this chapter, the bishops characterized young people as non-conformists who call everything into question. (These are considered positive traits.) They say that young people have a spirit of risk that can lead to radical commitment. They say that young people, too, have the creative capacity, the force, to bring about new responses to our changing world. Young people, they maintain, "wish to construct a better world and, sometimes without even knowing it, they are seeking the evangelical values of truth, justice and love" (DP 1131). Young people are characterized as signs of joy and happiness, very sensitive to social problems, and able to rebelliously reject a society that has grown full of hypocrisy and anti-Christian values (DP 1168).

Youth should be defined as an attitude toward life. In youth, we find a hope and desire for a better future. Youth are people of service and commitment, people who have new and different views of the world and the Church. Some young people love the Church. Some call it into question and demand that it be authentic. Some look for Christ but avoid involvement in the Church. Many of them are disturbed by social troubles and the world around them. "They look to the Church as a space of freedom, as a place where they can express themselves without being manipulated and engage in social and political protest" (DP 1180).

Many Hispanic young people today turn to the Church for fulfillment in their lives. But, if the Church does not have a sound youth ministry, they will be disappointed and disillusioned. A sound youth ministry will incorporate evangelized youth as helpers who give other young people the peer support they need. The Latin American Bishops' document *Pastoral Juvenil: Si a la Civilizacion de Amor* (*Youth Ministry: Yes to the Civilization of Love*) sees evangelization as being the operational component which will enable the Church to bring youth into itself so that, with the help of young people themselves, Church members will be able to reconstruct society into a more Christian environment.

Youth evangelization, therefore, is a particularly important aspect of a comprehensive pastoral ministry to Hispanic adolescents in that it is the door by which many young people are able to enter into the Church not simply as passive observers but as active members. Youth evangelization brings to pastoral ministry and the church the dynamism and the hope that only youth can contribute. I see this in ministry with La Tropa de Cristo in two particular ways. First, youth evangelization through the ministry of the Tropa has helped to bring many young people into personal encounters with the Living Christ. It has also brought them into personal encounter with the Church, the community of believers. Second, once young people have encountered both Christ and Christ's body, the Church, they become active members of the Christian community. Some become active by simply being better Christians in their homes, in their schools, and elsewhere. Others actually become active in ministry in their parishes. A few take on a call to direct evangelization through kerygmatic proclamation, like those who have joined La Tropa de Cristo.

Through the ministry of La Tropa de Cristo and the youth ministry program overall at our parish, Nuestra Senora de los Angeles, with evangelization being the heart and soul of the ministry, there are steps that lead young persons to the Kerygma Experience retreat and, then, toward a follow-up program that helps young persons grow in their experience of evangelization and move toward becoming evangelizers themselves, in one way or the other.

LA TROPA DE CRISTO

The development of La Tropa de Cristo was not something that I intended. When first sent to Neustra Senora de los Angeles, my interest was simply in doing parochial ministry. To tell you the truth, I had done only one year of youth ministry, back in the early '80s, as a Catholic high school teacher in Indianapolis. That experience was okay. But, in reality, I found I did not enjoy working with teenagers.

My experience with La Tropa de Cristo has changed all that. Upon my arrival at the parish, I was immediately sent to Mexico City to receive training in the area of evangelization. Upon my return, I got involved in adult evangelization and high school catechesis.

In August 1985, with the help of a team from Del Rio, Texas, our parish held its first two adult evangelization retreats. They were such successes that another retreat was scheduled for the end of September.

Fortunately for our parish, the Del Rio team was not able to give that adult retreat. We had to organize and form our own adult retreat team. I spent most of my ministry during 1985 and early 1986 focusing my attention on the development of adult evangelization communities and the training of people to do adult evangelization retreats.

In August 1985, our parish had a retreat for young people called "Y.E.S." It was done by a team from the parishes of El Carmen and St. Clare. The "Y.E.S." (Youth Evangelizing for the Savior) Retreat went well. But it was not as successful as the adult retreat. As far as youth were concerned, evangelization would then take the form of a catechetical program which would extend the talks from the adult evangelization retreat through the period of one school year. I gathered a group of young adults willing to work with me on this project. We would meet inside our church and give talks to all members of the student body. Then, students would be divided up for small group discussions.

In Fall, 1986, it was decided that we would do a follow-up course to help the students, who had been through their first year of evangelization, continue to grow in following Jesus Christ. But there was a problem. We had new students who had not yet experienced the Kerygma retreat and needed to do so before they could enter our high school program. It was decided that these students should attend an adult evangelization retreat.

One of the young people who made this retreat was Frank Gonzalez. Frank was an upbaptized sophomore at the time he made his first retreat. From what I can gather from his testimony, Frank's parents had decided not to baptize him but rather let him choose, when he was older, what Church he would like to attend. As a result, he had never attended any Church, unless it was to walk his grandmother to mass on Sunday. To hear Frank tell his story, every Sunday he would walk his grandmother to church and then stand outside and wait for her. When mass was over, he would walk her back home. One particular Sunday, however, it began to rain. Frank was forced to wait inside the church. At that time he heard the announcement for the evangelization retreat. And for some reason he felt compelled to sign up.

Once Frank had made his evangelization retreat he signed up for our catechetical program and joined in our first evangelization community. He also entered the RCIA process and began to move toward baptism. As part of his RCIA process, Frank was asked—along with another young lady by the name of Corina Esquivel—to help with an evangelization retreat. For the first time in our parish young people began to prepare themselves to do evangelization ministry. During this time, Frank likewise began to work on bringing his football buddies to the Church.

As I look back over the history of my involvement in youth evangelization I can see that it was Frank who laid the foundation for La Tropa de Cristo and chose the ministry of youth evangelization for me. At Easter 1987, Frank was baptized into the Church. I had the privilege of sponsoring him as his godfather. After that, slowly but surely, Frank began to bring to the Church other young people from Harlandale High School where he was a student. Frank was a football player. Other football players would notice that every Monday, after practice, Frank would not take time to shower. Instead he would run off as if he was in a hurry to get to somewhere important. A couple of football players asked, "Where do you go every Monday night all stinky and sweaty?" Frank said, "To Church." Before you knew it, we had a number of stinky, sweaty football players rushing in after football practice to be at our catechetical program. It was then that the interest in having an evangelization retreat specifically for youth arose.

Frank, Corina, and a few of the young adults who worked in the catechetical program helped put together our first youth evangelization retreat. Helping also on this retreat were four young women from Mexico who taught us that youth can be reached through the use of skits. Once the retreat was over, these four young ladies returned to Mexico. The kids on the retreat team began to work on a Living Stations of the Cross for the parish. During this time, we attended the Archdiocesan Super Youth Spectacular in San Antonio. We were surprised to see a group of young people called N.E.T. (National Evangelization Team) doing the entire conference. Our kids turned to each other and said, "We can do that." At that time, La Tropa de Cristo began to be.

Frank, Corina, Gen, Riq, Raquel and a few other people got together to form a one-time team to give our first real youth evangelization retreat, based on the SINE model. Our intention was that team members would give the retreat, then return to their communities. What happened instead was that the inspiration they had received from Youth Spectacular led them to form a permanent team. Soon the team was invited by the national SINE office to perform two half-hour dramas at the San Antonio Municipal Auditorium for a national conference on evangelization. We spent the whole summer of 1988 preparing for these two dramas entitled Santa Gasolina Catholic Church and La Joven Rica. Santa Gasolina was a spoof on what happens when a pastor tries to do everything in a traditional parish which was set as a gasoline station. La Joven Rica took the call of the disciples and Jesus' meeting with a rich young man and brought these stories into modern day San Antonio. In our story, the rich young person was female.

While preparing for the SINE Conference we came up with the name La Tropa de Cristo. My mother has always called a gang of people a *tropa*. Tropa is the Spanish word for an acting troupe. We were actors. So I naturally started calling the group Tropa. Others began to refer to it as Gilberto's Tropa. We wanted to emphasize that La Tropa belongs to Christ. We began to call ourselves La Tropa de Cristo. There were about twelve or thirteen of us in the original Tropa.

Our work at the national SINE Conference on evangelization was well received. Because of it, parishes in South Texas began to call on us to do conferences and retreats for their young people.

In October 1988, La Tropa de Cristo made its first missionary effort by going to do an evangelization retreat in Alice, Texas. Soon after, the Archdiocesan Office of Youth Ministry, in San Antonio, asked us to give a half-hour presentation at a youth ministry workshop for the western deaneries of the Archdiocese. These two events really got the ball rolling for us. We began to do all sorts of retreats, workshops, and conferences.

Tropa has changed and developed in the last couple of years. A major change began when we got four members of La Tropa to do full time ministry as Franciscan Servidores. Franciscan Servidores is a group of volunteer lay ministers working at Nuestra Senora de los Angeles. As part of its ministry, it directs the Tropa. At present, two Tropa members are Franciscan Servidores—Leroy (first year) and Brenda (second year).

Another major change has been that La Tropa has evolved from a youth evangelization team to a Franciscan evangelization team. This has helped members incarnate their religious beliefs in their everyday lives, especially through trying to live more simple lives, in purity and in commitment to the church parish.

I have been amazed at what the Holy Spirit can do. The Tropa de Cristo began as a group of youth and adults preparing to do a one-time only retreat. It has developed into a complete evangelization ministry that has taken us throughout the Archdiocese of San Antonio and has taken us as far away as the dioceses of Brownsville, El Paso, and up to Nebraska and Chicago. We have even had the privilege of addressing the issue of youth evangelization at the National Conference of Catholic Evangelization (NCCE) last year in Houston, Texas. Six years ago, when I first came to our parish, I never would have imaged that I would be doing this type of ministry and enjoying it.